M000077963

Love Like There's No Tomorrow is a beautifully encouraging book about the second (and third!) chances God grants us, and how he intersects our trauma with genuine grace. Poignant storytelling, raw honesty, and glimpses of God's plan—this book will remain with you.

—MARY DEMUTH, author of *Worth Living:*
How God's Wild Love for You Makes You Worthy

Ocieanna's dying wasn't the beginning nor the end of her story. The suffering of one moment has given her a clear vision of who she was, who God is, and what she is to do now. She reminds us that serving Christ isn't the same as knowing him, along with so many more lessons of love that will have me thinking and incorporating them for years—perhaps my entire life.

—PETER LEAVELL, author of *Gideon's Call*,
award-winning novelist, speaker, and historian

Ocieanna's personal journey of trials, emotional pain, and ultimate redemption will inspire you to look at yourself and others the way God does—like a child who is loved, like there's no tomorrow.

—ANNA DEBORD, mom of two

In the grips of a cardiac event, life becomes a vapor Ocieanna can't grab onto, drifting away from her grasp. In her book *Love Like There's No Tomorrow*, she describes the intensity a cardiac arrest has on everyone around her—and the residual effects it leaves forever. Through the experiences and stories she shares, her candor and openness transport the reader into a changed life and changed world. But the goal is clear: Ocieanna offers the privilege, discovery, and new life derived from her faith in Jesus. Cardiac arrest need not be fatal, but instead, a gateway to renewed love for life and our Creator.

—CINDY SCINTO, heart transplant recipient, speaker, teacher,
and author of *A Heart Like Mine* and *A Heart Like Yours*

There are few memoirs like this one. *Love Like There's No Tomorrow* is at once an exploration of our common human wounds, a vulnerable account of spiritual failings, very solid theology, triumphant, longing, hopeful. Young, old, rich, poor, alive or nearly dead, it is likely you'll find elements of your own story echoed in these pages. And it is certain you will find the grace of Jesus, which has clearly shaped every word.

—MATT BARKER, pastor, Grace Reformed Church, Walkerton, Indiana

God's faithfulness and healing is revealed in this inspiring true story. I was deeply moved by Ocieanna's openness and vulnerability in her memoir of love.

—HEIDI DALRYMPLE, homeschool mom of three

Love Like There's No Tomorrow taught me one thing above all else: he LOVES me. I can stop striving to please him by my works, worrying that he's frowning on me, or doubting his grace. He LOVES me. I will always be grateful for this book's reminder of that.

—CAROL PERLOT, entrepreneur and mom of two

If you're going through a struggle in life, whether emotional, physical, or financial, you should read *Love Like There's No Tomorrow*. It is a wonderful and wonder-filled book about how God works in our lives, especially in our trials. It's a reminder of how graciously he gives us second chances, and how he brings beauty from ashes. You will not be the same after reading this book.

—MARY STARMAN, product marketing and management maven

I thought this was going to be Ocieanna's story, but instead I found myself in the middle of my own story, which helped me to evaluate my own relationships with my immediate family, parents, and God. What wonderful reminders that each moment was orchestrated by God and that these relationships are a gift from Him and should be treated as such. Thank you for sharing your heart, Ocieanna!

—STEPHANIE JOHNSON, teacher and mom of four

Ocieanna provides insight into the most humbling of experiences in a way that takes the reader alongside her life-changing journey.

—ABBY RIEB, marketing manager, Christian Care Ministry

Love
like there's no
TOMORROW

HOW A CARDIAC ARREST
BROUGHT MY HEART TO LIFE

OCIEANNA FLEISS

BroadStreet
PUBLISHING

BroadStreet Publishing Group, LLC
Racine, Wisconsin, USA
BroadStreetPublishing.com

Love like there's no TOMORROW
How a Cardiac Arrest Brought My Heart to Life

ISBN-13: 978-1-4245-5142-2 (softcover)
ISBN-13: 978-1-4245-5143-9 (e-book)

Scripture quotations are taken from *The Holy Bible, English Standard Version* (ESV). Copyright © 2000; 2001 by Crossway Bibles, a division of Good News Publishers. Used by permission.

Cover design by Yvonne Parks at www.pearcreative.ca
Interior design and typeset by Katherine Lloyd at TheDESKonline.com

Printed in the United States of America

Dedication

This book is for my Ben, who watched his mom die.
I pray you'll always know the love of Christ.
I love you like there's no tomorrow.

Not to us, O Lord, not to us,
but to your name give glory for the sake of
your steadfast love and your faithfulness!
(Psalm 115:1)

CONTENTS

9

FOREWORD

This is a story of faithfulness—a testament of God's unceasing faithfulness toward those he loves. Prior to her medical crisis, Ocieanna Fleiss had no way of knowing what lay ahead of her or the challenges she would face. However, a life of following and depending on Christ prepared her and her family to weather a storm that hit them out of nowhere. The importance of being in fellowship and connected to other Christians is also a central theme. God truly knows what we need, and who we need, before we ever do.

From the prayers of a desperate husband watching powerlessly as the paramedics frantically tried to revive his wife, to the simple words uttered in confidence by a child who was trusting the Lord for a miracle, the Fleiss family was faithful. Their pastor and their church family were faithful. Their friends were faithful. And ultimately Christ was faithful.

Ocieanna's story is an extraordinary one, and while most of us will never face a life-and-death crisis like hers, the challenges of everyday life are ones to which we can all relate. Regardless of the severity of our struggles, through them all we see God's hand of healing, protection, and provision. We, at Medi-Share, were privileged to walk alongside Ocieanna on her medical journey, but we will always give God the glory for the fact that her fellow Medi-Share members shared her healthcare expenses. Our God is faithful, and He uses the faithfulness of His people to work in the lives of others to meet their needs.

Thank you, Ocieanna, for sharing your story. Seeing your faith lived out has been a blessing to all of us.

His kingdom come!

Tony Meggs
President & CEO, Christian Care Ministry

Let love and faithfulness never leave you; bind them around your neck, write them on the tablet of your heart. Proverbs 3:3

AUTHOR'S NOTE

Although events and people in this book are real, names and some minor details have been changed. In one case (with the pastor in the third chapter) I combined two characters into one to avoid confusion. Every emotion in this book is absolutely real.

Part One

MICHAEL'S STORY

Chapter One

THE MIDNIGHT HOUR

The snares of death encompassed me;
the pangs of Sheol laid hold on me.
(Psalm 116:3)

That Saturday in January, the day my wife died, was the best day our family had experienced in months. It was relaxing, fun, and family centered. I loved it, a pocket of peace between the holidays and the return to life's heavy busyness.

The scent of bacon and pancakes lingered through our home as we broke out the longed-for Wii that Ben, our ten-year-old, got for Christmas. We jumped around our messy family room playing tennis, boxing, and bowling.

Well, *I* didn't jump. I hobbled like a peg-legged pirate on my broken ankle. Three months before, I had slipped on wet grass in a sloped parking lot. Yeah, not that dramatic, but it sure impacted our life. Since I'd been laid off, I'd taken a commission-only job. Not bringing home income for three months—not good.

Gabrielle, my nine-year-old daughter, slammed her winning shot, then punched the air. "Ha! I beat you again."

I grabbed her and tickled her. "Hey, cut me some slack for my broken ankle."

Gabrielle donned a sassy grin. "That's not why you lost. You lost because I'm awesome!"

Ocieanna watched from the couch, with Christian, six, and Abigail, four, cuddled next to her.

"Okay, let me give it a try." Ocieanna broke away from the little ones and commandeered the controller. "But I want to bowl. C'mon, Ben."

"You're going to play? Cool!" Ben offered an excited grin. "I always love beating you, Mom."

"Hey, I was a master bowler in my day, I'll have you know."

"Yeah, right." Ben switched the game.

"But it's my turn!" Abigail protested.

"No, it's not," Christian said. "You played twice. I had only one turn. Gabby beat Papa twice. And Ben gets to play because it's his game."

"Whatever, Christian." Abigail's chin quivered. Tears sprouted from her eyes. "I never get to play."

"Don't worry, honey." I scooched in next to her. She climbed onto my lap and popped her thumb in her mouth, content.

Ben beat Ocieanna at bowling, and then pizza around the kitchen table bookended the memorable day. I offered thanks for the food. "Heavenly Father, thank you for my family. Thank you for this time together."

As Ocieanna tucked the kids into bed, I heard her singing, and I paused, listening to my wife shower love on our children. I'd spied a light in her hazel eyes today, a joy I hadn't seen in a long time. Normally she wore stress like a leaden coat, wearing her down. I parked on the bed and my broken ankle throbbed as I slid off the medical "boot" that kept my bones in line. The cool air made my wrinkled, damp skin tingle. I hated that Ocieanna had to work so hard, but what could we do? We couldn't possibly survive without her income.

Ocieanna shut the door to Christian's room as I stretched the ball of my foot as far forward as the implanted metal posts would allow. Then I twisted it back, cringing at the pain but enjoying the freedom of movement. Gingerly, I lobbed my still-swollen hoof onto the bed. On Monday, I'd have a quick surgery to remove the metal pins. Then life would get back to normal. As soon as I could catch up with the work I'd missed.

She walked in and unclasped her hair from its ponytail. It spilled down her back and I marveled again at how beautiful she was. I longed for her to hurry. Get ready for bed. Be with me. But I kept my hopes to myself. Work constantly pressured her. She might have to retreat to her computer tonight. I lay back, waiting.

"Hey," she softly said.

My heart wavered as she moved toward me, sat on the edge of the bed, and massaged the muscles around my sore ankle. She tilted her head and snagged my eyes with her gaze. "Do you want to watch something tonight?"

"Really? You don't have to work?"

At the word *work*, gloominess fell over her face, but only momentarily. "I will have to get back to editing on Monday, but tonight I want to be with you."

I stared at her, studying her. Her eyes seemed relaxed, loving. A thrill coursed through me. She hadn't looked at me like that in a long time. She didn't allow herself time to feel. Maybe that was my fault, for pushing her to work so much.

After changing into her nightgown, she snuck to the bed and laid her head against my chest. Her breathing slowed to a rhythmic pace as she relaxed. I felt her heart beating next to mine. I cherished her soft hand on my skin, the smell of her hair.

About a half hour passed, and she wormed to her side of the bed. Still engrossed in the show, she reached for my hand, caressed my arm.

We watched together, in silence. Weariness lingered nearby, pulling me toward blissful sleep. Ocieanna's eyes drooped.

Thank you, Lord.

But then as a character in the show gasped as if dying, Ocieanna made a similar sound. Ha. Maybe she wasn't so near to falling asleep. I thought she was mocking the character.

But she didn't stop.

"Darlin'?"

Within half a moment, I knew something was wrong, but what? A seizure?

Her labored breathing increased until it was a gravelly rasping. My heart raced. Her back arched, her mouth opened, and her eyes rolled up. The subtle birthmark on her neck glowed a violent purple. What was happening? Her face was turning pale. She reached for her throat, her fingers curling like stiff branches.

Fear lit and blazed through me, igniting me to action.

"Ocieanna!" I tried to wake her, but she wasn't responding. I slapped her face, once, twice. It didn't work. She kept gasping. I veered toward surrendering to an overpowering panic, but the kids in their bedrooms—I couldn't freak out. I had to stay strong for them.

And Ocieanna—her life seemed to be in my hands. Could I save her? What should I do? This question pounded on the door of my thoughts as snarled emotions stormed, tossing me on a sea with no way to steer.

And then her raspy wheezing stopped.

The silence was much worse. Alarm coursed through every cell in my body, but I fought it. I had to save my wife. She would die if I didn't act. She was already dead.

"Darlin'!" I yelled again, now more of a begging than expecting her to respond. I did what I'd learned as a child and strove to breathe life back into her, an attempt at mouth to mouth. Nothing. Sometime in the midst of this Ben faltered in. My boy stood motionless, staring at his mom who wasn't moving.

I yelled at him, shocking him alert. "Get the phone!"

Ben raced down the stairs and then charged back up to our bedroom. Terror engraved his face, which was pale despite his spurt of exercise.

I grabbed the phone from Ben and dialed 911. While I waited, I ordered, "Make sure the kids' doors are closed. Unlock the front door."

Ben's blue eyes, full of panic, focused on his mission. Then he rushed away.

The 911 operator answered. "What's your emergency?"

"My wife. She's not breathing."

After taking more information, she asked, "Are you giving her CPR?"

"I'm trying."

"Okay, an ambulance is on the way. Here's what you need to do ..."

She talked me through CPR. She said not to do the mouth to mouth, but to focus on chest compressions. One, two, three, four, five ... to one hundred. With every pump, I begged, *Please God. Please. Please. Please.*

"Okay, I got it," I said. "I'm going to hang up."

But she wanted to stay on the line with me. I struggled to pump and count and hold the phone. It felt insane. *Let me hang up!* I didn't care about the woman on the phone. I needed to focus on Ocieanna.

We finished one hundred compressions. "Okay, start over," she said. "You're doing great." Her words furnished no comfort.

"Don't go, darlin'. Don't leave me."

The operator stayed on the line as we counted together to two hundred, three hundred, four hundred. Still no response in Ocieanna's body. She was limp, not moving. The intense fear blended with sharp pangs of grief. *She's slipping from me.*

Her face turned blueish white.

Five hundred pumps.

"Oh, darlin', come back to me!"

Minutes after I called, though it seemed like forever, the lights from ambulances glowed through our window. I heard Ben let the paramedics in. They stormed up the stairs and into my room, carrying machines, bags, a gurney.

A frigid January chill entered with them.

A tall, thin man asked, "How old is she?" He didn't look at me, but focused on Ocieanna.

"Forty-two." I stepped back as another man and a woman lifted her from the bed and laid her on the floor.

"Any medications?"

"None that I know of."

A man kicked open the bathroom door to make room. Another set up a defibrillator.

The first man spoke into a radio. "Forty-two-year-old woman. No known medications. Apparent cardiac arrest."

More paramedics rushed in.

Cardiac arrest? Ocieanna had a cardiac arrest? What did that even mean? I stepped back, out of the fray, and in those short moments, sobs clawed at my throat. I wanted to weep, to scream, to cling to my wife. But I held it all back. I wouldn't lose it. The kids. The kids. The kids.

Each medic performed a vital task—all geared toward reviving my darlin's dead body. One ripped off her pajama top. Another inserted an IV.

Two paramedics hooked her up to monitors. Erratic spikes and drops on the monitor displayed the only sign she'd been alive. I had felt her limp body. She was gone. How long? Five minutes? Ten minutes? I couldn't be sure. In a moment, even these residual electrical impulses slowed, stilled to a flatline.

Overcome with shock, I felt numb. I couldn't believe the reality screaming at me. I studied her still body. It was almost peaceful, like a body in a casket. *She's dead. Ocieanna's gone.*

My thoughts flashed to the idea of being a single dad. What would we do without her? How would I tell the little ones? Thank God they weren't seeing this.

The paramedics stuck the tabs of the defibrillator onto her chest. After a moment, the machine spoke. "Please stand clear." A feminine mechanical voice. "Push button."

I held my breath. This would get her heart going again. It had to. Everything would be okay.

The woman pushed the button, then we collectively waited in stilted silence as the machine shocked my wife. Her arms flinched, her torso jerked upward, but she didn't cough and start breathing like in the movies.

No change in the monitor. Still a flatline.

My heart sank to my stomach.

The tall paramedic instructed them to reset the defibrillator. His eyes—all their eyes—showed intense focus.

After less than a second the machine beeped, and again the mechanical voice said, "Please stand clear. Push button."

Every muscle in me tensed. *Come back, darlin'.*

The machine shocked her. The same jerking.

Still no response. No change.

The paramedics, still so focused, also displayed worry. I couldn't wake her. Neither could they. Was that it? Was this over? Would they give up now?

The room around me became a blur. I heard rustling, footsteps, and muffled words, but couldn't focus. Outwardly I remained calm, but inside, torrents of panic raged. All I could think was I'd lost her. *Ocieanna's gone. My wife. My best friend. My girl.*

They tried again.

The machine spoke a third time. "Please stand clear. Push button." Her torso jerked. Her arms twitched, like before. And like before, she didn't cough and wake up. I saw no signs of breathing. No signs of life. My legs felt weak. A rancid heat rose from my stomach to my aching head. I almost collapsed, but then ...

"I have a pulse!" the tall man shouted, and immediately the room burst with activity.

"Oh my God," I cried out. Through tears, I inspected the monitor. The line now moved with small jagged rises and falls, but it was moving.

I stumbled over my broken ankle and had to grab the wall to steady myself. Was she really okay? Her heart beat again. I battled to hold onto that, but uncertainty crept in. I wanted to feel relieved, but fear—so strong—brought doubt. Her body had lain still for so long.

In quick moments, they inserted a respiratory bag to manually breathe for her, secured her body, and loaded her onto the gurney. I found security in the paramedics' decisive speed, such a contrast to my earlier confusion.

Less than a half hour after I first heard her gasping, they rushed her down the stairwell. My mind and emotions raced to catch up with reality. *Did this really happen?* As they transported her through our sage-green living room, I scrutinized Ocieanna—long waves of light-brown hair, bunched behind her head, eyes closed, arms and legs motionless, respiratory bag disfiguring her mouth. Was this really my beautiful, vibrant wife? I yearned to retreat to the moments when she caressed my arm as we watched TV. When our gazes linked as she crawled into bed. Could my life fall apart this quickly? How could it be true?

I posted myself at the bottom of the stairs. Ben found me. He was crying, spewing sobs. I enclosed him next to me.

The team of medics didn't pause for us to say good-bye, to touch her. We observed helplessly as she passed through the door and into the ambulance. One by one the first responders climbed into their vehicles, turned off their flashing lights, and disappeared into the darkness. The head paramedic remained—the tall, thin one who had asked the questions.

"Well, we've got a heartbeat. For now."

I clutched Ben to my side. "What do you mean, 'for now'?"

"Not many people survive the trauma she's been through." He looked at Ben. "You need to be prepared. Your mom may not come home."

Ben and I gawked at the man. *Why would you tell him that?* I thought, already powerless to comfort my son.

"I'm sorry. You may want to follow us in a few minutes. We'll be taking her to Valley."

I nodded, appreciating him and his crew but at the same time wanting the last intruder to leave my home. I shut the door behind him, and with Ben beside me, I watched as Ocieanna was driven away, not certain if I'd spent my last moments with my wife.

Chapter Two

THE DEAD OF NIGHT

In my distress I called upon the LORD;
to my God I cried for help.
From his temple he heard my voice,
and my cry to him reached his ears.
(Psalm 18:6)

en and I continued gazing out the window, dazed. The night, both inside and outside, loomed dark, quiet now, as if sucked of life. A wave of grief struck me, like a violent gale in an ice storm. Fear attacked my throat at the finality of death. I longed to run from this truth, to deny the fact that Ocieanna would probably die, but I forced myself to wrestle with it, to hold on to the fear, to let the freezing pain numb me.

I had to. The unrealistic hope that reached toward me, like a rescuer's hand, terrified me even more. If I hoped—as I longed to—that Ocieanna would survive, the disappointment afterward would destroy me. I knew this. The truth resided in those ten minutes. She hadn't moved for *ten minutes*. Her body had been cold beneath my hands, my lips. It was futile to hope she'd be okay. So instead, I focused on preparing myself to be strong for the kids. They would need me.

"C'mon, Ben." I rubbed his back as we knelt before the green couch. I folded my hands like a child. Ben did too.

I couldn't pray my heart—I would break down, and Ben needed me—so I prayed stiffly, words I knew I should say and wanted to believe. "Heavenly Father, if it's your will, please bring Ocieanna home. We know you're with us, even now. Help us to trust you, no matter what happens."

After these words, I bided in silence a moment as God's presence enveloped me. He accepted my weak attempt at prayer. My wife was going to die. This reality, which all the facts screamed, terrified me. But in my broken anguish, I also knew God was with me. No great theological truth, no wise sermon, no memorable hymn lyrics comforted me in that moment. Just "I will be with you."

Finally, my mind reeled back to the puzzle before me. What to do next? Would I have to wake the other kids, take them to the hospital with me? Should I call someone?

A knock on the door interrupted these thoughts. It was Cynthia, our neighbor, asking if she could help. "I saw the ambulances."

I could hear my voice shake as I told her what happened.

Her shoulders slumped, as if in shocked disbelief. "I just saw her get the mail today. We chatted ..." She sighed. "Are you going to the hospital? I'll stay with the kids."

"Yes. Thank you."

"Where are they?"

I glanced around. Other than making sure their doors were shut, I hadn't checked on them. "They must still be asleep."

Her eyes widened. "They slept through paramedics racing up and down the stairs right next to their doors?"

A sense of awe filled me. "I don't know how, but they didn't wake up."

"That's amazing." Her voice softened with compassion. "I'll sack out on the couch until you get back. Don't worry about the kids."

"Thank you, Cynthia."

I turned to Ben and cupped his head in my hands. "We're going to the hospital, bud. Get dressed."

As I drove, I had Ben dial, and then I put my Bluetooth in as it rang. It was almost 1 a.m., but I didn't hesitate to make this call. "Pastor Barker ... uh ... Matt? I'm sorry to call so late. Ocieanna's in the hospital."

"What?" the associate pastor of our conservative Presbyterian church asked groggily.

I fought to be strong. "They think she had a cardiac arrest. She's at Valley Medical Center."

"A cardiac arrest? That's not possible."

I explained the events of the night, feeling like I relayed someone else's story. This couldn't be happening to us—to me.

"Be right there. I'll send out a prayer e-mail to the church first. And, brother, I'm praying."

I drove through the wooded darkness toward the hospital, and my heart wavered between trying to trust God and crushing fear.

Pastor Barker's praying. Others will be soon. God is with us. God is with us.

At about 1:30, Ben and I warily strode across the parking lot. I wanted to rush to see Ocieanna, but I also hesitated, my stomach knotted. What would they tell me? Did Ocieanna survive the ambulance ride? Ben grasped my hand, hugged my arm as we strode under the electric illumination from the streetlights.

When we reached the glass door of the emergency room, I couldn't help but remember another time Ocieanna and I had arrived through this door late at night. Past her due date, we'd waited too long to go to the hospital. She was hunched over with

29

intense nonstop contractions, moaning and crying. How helpless I felt, wanting to stop her suffering yet proud of my amazing wife. The mother of my children.

They rushed her to labor and delivery, then twenty minutes later, she held our youngest child in her arms, sweet Abigail. Ocieanna never looked more beautiful as I kissed her forehead, gazed into her eyes. We shared a moment, a connection of awe and love and thankfulness. We'd had two miscarriages before having kids, so each birth seemed amazing, remarkable—worthy of our most heartfelt praise. Out of loss came the light of adoration, and out of these beams flowed unbounded joy.

Holding our tiny bundle of life, I couldn't believe how blessed I was to have Ocieanna. As hard as parenting was at times, I could do it—providing we journeyed together.

How different this night felt.

I grabbed the door's cold metal handle, but it wouldn't budge. I jerked it, and it rattled against the lock. They must've installed new security measures. My heart raced with frustration. I couldn't bear even the slightest obstacle. I would break. Irrational panic rose as I shook the door. Ben gazed up at me, and then a nurse inside spotted us, frowned, and pointed toward a communicator on the wall. Suddenly embarrassed, I lowered my head as she buzzed us in.

"My wife was brought here," I said, approaching her desk. "Ocieanna Fleiss."

The young African American woman didn't look at us as her fingernails clicked on the keyboard. Then her eyes rounded, and she let out an almost unnoticeable gasp. She lost her angry frown, her forehead creasing in concerned empathy. Her compassion felt like a punch, and I liked the frustrated frown better. "They're taking care of her," she said gently. "I'll get you checked in."

After a too-long process of filling out forms and donning wrist bands, she finally directed us to the family waiting room.

We crossed through the door into the room's false warmth and contrived comfort. I imagined designers trying to pick the most comforting colors, muted tones, lighting. The couch and chairs perfectly suited the mood of the room yet failed to invite emotion. I couldn't picture someone falling down in tears on the taupe pleather. The room communicated *Hold yourself together. Everything's comfortable. Nothing's sad.* I wondered how many other families had huddled in this room, what news they'd heard. "Grandma made it through her surgery." "I'm sorry, your daughter lost too much blood ..." What news would I hear?

"The doctor will talk to you when he's ready," the woman said as she turned to leave.

"Can we see her first?"

She paused, laid a hand on my arm, and I bristled. I didn't want this stranger's compassion. I wanted Ocieanna.

"I'm sorry," she said. "Not right now."

The sterile scent of rubbing alcohol wafted in as we waited alone. A TV hung from the ceiling in a corner, tuned to CNN, yet with the volume turned down and subtitles flashing across the mute news anchors' faces.

Ben shivered, and I pulled him next to me, smoothed his hair. "I love you."

With a stifled sob, Ben burrowed his head into my chest. My son needed his dad. Eager to be there, holding him, I found purpose in fathering him. And his presence comforted me too. Waiting wordlessly, I strained to hear signs of the doctor coming. Muffled voices spoke of medications and patients. Doors opened and closed. Footsteps approached, but no one came.

Warily, Ben sat up. "I've been saying memory verses to myself."

I rubbed Ben's shoulder. "Oh, bud, that's the perfect thing to do. Which ones?"

"The Lord is my shepherd."

Together, we quoted, "The Lord is my shepherd. I shall not want … yea though I walk through the valley of the shadow of death, I will fear no evil, for you are with me."

You are with me …

The door opening interrupted our time. Pastor Barker entered. He was casually dressed in jeans and a T-shirt, his hair skewed from sleep probably, unshaved—but a good sight. In my heart I sensed a visible picture of Christ, loving us at this moment, sending his shepherd to care for us in the dark of night. At the sight of him, sobs erupted, but I constricted them back down, making it hard to breathe. I stood and reluctantly received a hug, uncomfortable with physical displays of compassion, even from him. Pastor Barker embraced Ben too.

"The church is praying," was all he said, but his eyes held questions.

"We're okay," I started. "They haven't told us anything about Ocieanna yet."

The door squeaked open again. Laury, a dear friend's daughter, glided in. An emergency room nurse dressed in scrubs, she'd obviously been on duty for a while. I'd known her since she was a young teenager, remembered her hard years in nursing school.

She threw us a questioning look. "Pastor Barker? Hey, Michael. Hey, Ben. What are you guys doing here?"

I squeezed Ben's shoulder. "Ocieanna was brought in about twenty minutes ago. They think she had a …" I swallowed. "A cardiac arrest."

Color emptied from Laury's face, revealing concern, almost panic. "What? That was Ocieanna? I saw … I didn't know it was her." Her hands shook, her eyes welled with tears. "I'm sorry." She pivoted toward the door. "I have to go."

What were these medical people not telling me?

Ben eyed me. "What's wrong with Miss Laury? Dad, is Mom … gone?"

The door had barely closed behind Laury when a nurse arrived and took us to a long barren room with no windows and two doors. Medical equipment lined the walls and a four-foot-high machine, with tubes flowing in and out, hummed at the other end of the room. Monitors stood guard around it, blocking like a parapet.

It took a moment before I realized Ocieanna was encased between the machines like Snow White. She wore a blue vest that received the gray tubes. The room felt like a morgue.

A doctor progressed toward us, skimming a clipboard. His white hair appeared disheveled, and his bushy dark eyebrows furrowed as he glanced up. "Mr. Fleiss?" He reached out his hand and shook mine. Without waiting for a response, he continued. "Your wife suffered a severe cardiac arrest." His stern eyes fixed on the chart, strictly professional.

"A heart attack?" I asked, mostly in shock.

"No." His unemotional voice slowed. "A sudden cardiac arrest. There's a difference. You can look it up. The odds aren't good. Nationally, only five percent of cardiac arrest victims survive. Here in King County that goes up to twenty percent due to our emphasis on cardiac health. Since your wife is only forty-two, I'll give her a fifty percent chance." He sprayed these cold facts on me as if from a fire hose—tons of suffocating water per second. Then he paused, waiting for a reaction.

Too astonished to formulate an answer, I searched his face blankly. *This is the rudest, most curt doctor I've ever met.*

The terse healer dropped a pen in his coat pocket, then continued. "Right now we're keeping her in the coma. We're cooling her blood—that's what the vest and tubes are for. We'll chill her to the low 90s and then begin to slowly reheat the blood. We'll see what we're working with at that time. Even after the blood has warmed, we don't know if she'll come out of the coma. Sometimes even if they do survive, they never come out of a vegetative state. The coma and cooling may minimize brain damage, but her brain went without oxygen for a long time. If she does survive, you shouldn't expect her to be fully functional."

The doctor left, and I glanced at Pastor Barker. "What did he say?"

Pastor Barker tried to slowly explain, but it still barely registered. One thing kept coming back.

"Did he say five percent?"

Pastor Barker shook his head, then spoke calmly, gently. "Nationally, only five percent survive. It's twenty percent here in King County. He gave Ocieanna a fifty-fifty chance …"

Not a drop of comfort arose from those statistics. Five percent? Twenty? Fifty? None implied what I longed to hear: *Don't worry. Ocieanna's going to be okay.*

The sparse room's white walls towered around me. She seemed far away, as if a huge ravine separated her from me. They chilled her body. She hated being cold. I ached to warm her, save her, but I couldn't. My mind rushed to the chill of death. Would Ocieanna grow even colder? Would her dead body rest under the icy January soil? Would I feel her warm skin next to mine ever again?

Standing beside me, Ben studied Ocieanna. His breaths rose and fell, punctuating the terror in his eyes. In a soft voice, he said, "Love you, Mom," and tears trickled down his cheek. "Love you."

I kissed my son's head as Pastor Barker stepped forward, placed his hands on our backs, and prayed. I don't remember his words, but I felt love, as if his prayer represented Jesus himself interceding for us. The odd contrast of the moment settled over me—to be covered with this shelter of heavenly peace as Ocieanna's life was sustained by unnatural machines. The mechanical hums of fans and motors, the breathing machine, the blinks and pulsing lights became the setting for a desperate, heartbroken worship of the only one who could help. The only one who could comfort.

As the prayer finished, a new thought flickered in my mind. *If she was going to die, wouldn't she have passed in those first moments?* The doctor or nurse didn't say anything about this. It was a logical deduction I made, and held onto, in my ignorance. A tiny spark of hope.

Not wanting to get Ben's hopes up, I didn't say this out loud.

I noticed the clock on the wall. 3:25. My thoughts jumped to the kids at home—my three whose heads rested on their pillows with no idea their precious mama had died for ten minutes tonight, might never kiss them again, laugh with them, hug them. A strong urge to go home arrested me. I had to take care of my children. But how could I leave Ocieanna? I studied her face, looking so different, with the machines sustaining her. I inspected Ben, red-eyed and weary. Just a boy, he needed the stability of home, the comfort of the familiar. We both needed rest.

A nurse walked in—a young brown-haired woman. Her name tag read Alexandra. She grabbed Ocieanna's chart from its hook on the wall.

"Excuse me," I said. "Is anything likely to change in the next few hours? I mean, she's not going to …"

Alexandra finished reading the chart and then lifted her eyes toward me. "She should be good for a while." She spoke with a Russian accent. "We'll keep cooling her." She glanced at Ben, then back to me, and a blanket of compassion softened her brow, her shoulders. "You can go home. Get rest. Come back in the morning." She paused as if waiting for another question.

I shifted awkwardly, unsettled by the kindness in her gaze. "Thank you."

"You gave CPR?"

Those moments of pumping on Ocieanna's chest, pleading for her life, glared like forever ago. I nodded.

"You saved her life."

"I don't know." I fumbled for words. I wanted to collapse into tears. "I did what I could," I managed to say. Was it enough?

I turned to Pastor Barker. "I should get Ben home." A sick heartache formed. "Be there when the other kids wake up. Tell them."

Pastor Barker nodded. "Yeah. I'll tell the church this morning."

"Oh, that's right. It's Sunday."

I gazed across the room's long chasm. "We'll be back, darlin'."

"Good-bye, Mama."

"The sky's changing color," I said absently as we strode through the parking lot. "Sun'll be up soon."

Chapter Three

A BROKEN MORNING

Bear one another's burdens,
and so fulfill the law of Christ.
(Galatians 6:2)

I forced myself to hide in the silence of sleep for a couple hours after returning home at 4 a.m. Yet, soon my eyes jolted open, reality invading sleep's quiet forgetfulness. Rolling to my side, as gray light hampered my vision, I could imagine Ocieanna on her part of the bed. She should be there, sleeping, her lovely shape full of potential energy, unconsciously waiting to be the manager of our day, the lover of my children, the wife of my youth.

Was she really gone? Did last night truly happen?

I stretched my hand, touching her pillow, and then pulled it beneath my head, breathing her. So strange, unreal, that she'd been ripped away from me by death's desperate attempt to take her. Sobs welled, tears forced their way out. Did death still seek her life? Would God rescue her? Rescue me?

I inhaled and straightened. I couldn't give in to the temptation to wallow in my own distress. The kids would be up soon. They would race in, expecting a loving hug from their mama. I didn't want them to see the empty bed, not without talking to them first. The idea of what I had to do stirred sick agony in my stomach. I had no idea how I would tell my children that their mama might never come home. But this morning, I had a job. I was their father. Their buffer. Only me.

So I offered a quick prayer for help, rose, threw on my robe, and plodded down the hallway. Gabrielle was first. "Time to wake up."

She was our heaviest sleeper, so she mumbled and moaned. Then suddenly her brown eyes focused on me. "Where's Mama? You never wake us up."

I should've known my dark-haired Gabrielle would sense something was wrong. "Meet me downstairs," I said, avoiding her question. "I'll be right there."

Christian and Abigail cheerfully made their way downstairs as I pulled Ben aside. His dirty-blond hair skewed as he leaned his head next to my middle.

"Don't say anything to the kids, okay?"

His lower lip quivered. "I understand."

I found the four of them spread throughout the family room. An abandoned Wii controller lay on the floor in front of the TV. Huddling onto the blue couch, I called them to me. My youngest pair, Christian and Abigail, snuggled onto my lap. I wrapped my arms around these two, feeling wisps of their silky dark hair against my neck. I observed Gabrielle, wary, worried, as she scooted next to me. Ben sank down on my other side. Terrified Ben.

As I drew them close, my kids became more precious to me than ever before. More importantly, all my other responsibilities became a fuzzy background, and only they—my family—stayed in focus. The recesses of my soul seared with intense love for them, and I thought this must be a glimpse of what the Father feels for his children.

I took in a breath and attempted to mask my lurking fear.

Gabrielle read me and pushed back against her spot on the

couch. "Something's wrong, Papa." Her voice was intense. "Tell us. Where's—"

"Oh, yeah," Abigail piped in. "Where's Mama? Is she getting ready for church?"

"Shush, Abigail." Gabrielle glared at her.

I could see this was already spiraling. I touched Gabrielle's cheek. Our eyes connected. "Yes, sweetie, something's wrong with Mama."

"What?" Christian jolted up. "What do you mean something's wrong with her? Isn't she here?"

"No, bud."

Little Abigail smoothed my hair from my forehead, her bright eyes gazing into mine. "Where is she?"

"God is with us, kids," I said slowly, cautiously, hoping to level the way. "Remember the verse about the shepherd?"

"We're his sheep, and God's the shepherd who kills the lions, like King David did," Abigail answered.

"With a rock and a slingshot!" Christian pretended to whirl a sling.

"Stop it!" Ben grabbed his arm, halting him. "Let Dad talk."

Christian wrenched his arm from Ben and slumped back down, shaking the rest of us on the sofa.

I placed a hand on Ben's shoulder and felt his muscles relax. Then I inhaled and surveyed the others. "Tell me more about the shepherd."

"It's Jesus! He loves us." Abigail beamed, always so confident in God's care. "I want to hug him."

Her joy grated on my stinging emotions, but I donned a smile. "That's right. Our shepherd loves us, no matter what."

Gabrielle jerked her head toward me, her body stiff, her deep-brown eyes narrow with concern. "Please, Papa! I don't care about the shepherd. What's wrong with Mama?"

Helplessness created a savage sorrow in my heart. My attempts to soften my kids' suffering only added to their anxiety. What was I thinking? How could I prepare them to possibly lose their mother? Nothing could.

I inhaled a shaky breath, let it out, then spoke the words I longed to avoid. "Mama had a cardiac arrest last night. It's like a heart attack."

"But worse," Ben added.

"The ambulances took her to the hospital." I reached over and held Ben's hand. "Ben and I went, too, to check on her."

"Ambulances?" Christian's eyebrows pushed up

"Yeah. Remember when we visited the fire station and the paramedics let us look inside?"

He slid from my lap to his knees and looked at me. "One came here?"

"A bunch, like twenty." Irritation tinged Ben's voice. I wondered how mixed up his emotions must have been—concern for his siblings blended with his own fear and weariness.

Christian placed his chubby hand on my arm. "Wait, so Mama's in the hospital?"

"Yes, bud."

His shoulders drooped, and he played with his sock.

Abigail's big eyes gazed up at me, full of trust. "When can we see her, Papa?"

"Today, honey. First, we're going to church. We need it." My voice softened. "I need it."

"I'll make Mama a picture of a butterfly," Abigail said. "Mama loves my pictures."

"Yes, she does." My throat burned. I could barely speak. "She won't be awake though. Right now, she's in a coma."

"What's a coma?" Christian's eyebrows creased.

Gabrielle, who now perched on the side of the sofa, stared out the window, its cloud-filtered light paling her cheek. "It means she's asleep and she can't wake up," she said. The words broke her, and she collapsed into sobs. "People don't wake up from comas. She's going to die. Isn't she, Papa?" Her shoulders heaved as tears streamed down her cheeks.

I moved to her and gathered her in my arms, her grief wetting my chest.

"Of course not. God's taking care of her." Abigail hugged Gabrielle's back, and then Christian joined in. Ben stood and walked out of the room.

Gabrielle searched my face. "Papa?"

Oh, Lord, if I could tell her that Mama will be okay. But I wouldn't lie. I held her damp cheeks in my hands. "I don't know. She could die. She's very sick."

Getting ready for church on the morning after my Ocieanna nearly died—still could die—felt agonizingly off. Helping the kids to wash, dress, and eat without Ocieanna managing our tasks. Not hearing her voice throughout the house. Not smelling her floral scent—lotion, I guess. Not walking into the warm bathroom after her steamy shower. Each of these gaps sucked my spirit dry.

I wore casual clothes, too tired—distracted—to think about a matching tie and shirt. Besides, Ocieanna always helped me with that. Gabrielle had fed the kids toast. They dressed themselves. Who knew if their outfits coordinated. Their hair may have been brushed—if Gabrielle and Ben helped—but I don't remember. I didn't care.

What I cared about was going to church. I loaded the kids in the van, and as if it were a shelter from a raging storm, I concentrated on getting to God's house. We drove in silence. To keep from falling apart, I focused my thoughts in a familiar realm—the

41

practical. How would I take care of the kids? How would I get Ben to his private school in the morning? Who would homeschool the little ones? What would we eat? I couldn't cook more than a can of chili. So much to figure out, but I would rather think about these particulars than … the other thought that loomed in the darkness.

I lumbered through the church's glass door and smelled the coffee brewing, noticed the familiar background chatting. My shoulders relaxed, slightly. The kids paused too. But as I scanned the people, I spotted many surprised faces.

"You're here," one man said as he hovered nearer. "During Sunday school they announced what happened. I'm so sorry. I don't know if I could've made it to church."

A quick stab of doubt about coming hit but immediately vanished. Where else would I go? I hungered for the love of God's people. My soul groaned to hear the gospel of grace and to be reminded that my Savior captained the boat through this tempest and would deliver me safely through. Plus, I was impelled to show my kids that when the worst happened, the place to turn wasn't to our pillows—to cry—but to Jesus.

I shrugged, and the man wandered away.

We meandered through the earth-toned foyer toward the sanctuary, and my kids' favorite babysitter, Miss Hannah, approached. She smiled compassionately, then knelt down and hugged the kids.

"C'mon, let's sit down," she said.

Like an angel sent to rescue me, she took their hands and led them to our usual row.

As they disappeared through the entrance to the sanctuary, I realized one problem about being at church. Being around these folks who loved us, who wanted to show compassion, could break the dam I was fighting so hard to keep strong.

As I paused, speculating, my friend Norm, a California transplant like us, met me and shook my hand. He knew better than to hug me. He didn't ask any questions or offer advice, just, "Love you, brother." Even at those slight words of comfort, my chin trembled. But I stuffed the emotion.

The service began, so I sat down on the familiar cushioned chair. I let my eyelids fall, relishing the momentary solitude. Then I filled my lungs with air and prayed the words I kept repeating. *Lord, help us. Help Ocieanna. Help. Help. Help.* Abigail quietly climbed on my lap, but she accidentally kicked Christian's stomach in the process.

"Hey! You kicked me," Christian complained, way too loud.

Abigail sneered at him. "I didn't mean to. Geez."

I could feel an argument brewing. They were holding in so many emotions that this small argument could easily erupt into a huge mess.

Ben glared at them and then spoke through clenched teeth. "Stop it, you guys. Just stop!" I grasped what he was really saying: *I want you to be quiet. I'm sad and I need this time.* I felt the same.

Somehow, I settled them down, and Christian leaned against my arm. Ben stayed stiffly silent, and Gabrielle hung her head, her brown hair shrouding her face, quietly weeping. I don't think she had stopped crying all morning. I reached my arm over and held her shuddering shoulder.

I scanned the sanctuary—the window in the front, the wood paneling, the pulpit. All my memories of this place involved Ocieanna. I remembered when the church met in a school, and we and her parents—now passed—first became members. We were young, excited to serve the Lord in this body.

I skipped ahead to when Ocieanna held our oldest, Ben, days old, in her arms. She kissed his head as she handed him to the pastor to be baptized, marked as belonging to God. Ocieanna had always been at my side here. What if she never sat next to me again? What if—

Dangerous thoughts crept up, but I forced them away.

I listened to the Westminster Confession reading and the first hymns, barely taking them in … but then the sermon. Unbelievably, it was about serving one another, and at the end our pastor sent out a call to the congregation to help us.

As the service ended, I realized how weary I was. I had barely slept, ran on adrenaline. Yet a peace covered me in that moment. The peace like a river that steadily flowed, despite my squalling fear and emotion. A peace that didn't depend on me.

"Michael?" a voice stirred me. It was one of the deacons.

I didn't answer, just looked at him.

"I, uh, wanted to let you know that we had a meeting this morning about how to help you."

"The deacons?"

"No, I mean the whole church, during the Sunday school hour. It just sort of happened. Everyone wanted to help." He pulled out piece of paper. "We have people signed up to help with meals."

"Thank you so much," I said.

But he didn't stop. He showed me a second page, and a third. "We also have your homeschooling taken care of for two weeks. After that, we'll figure out what to do. One family has offered to pay a house-cleaning company. Three ladies signed up to do laundry. Kim will drive Ben to school. Is there anything else you might need?"

I shook my head, unable to speak.

He hunted my face, surely seeing the tears welling in my eyes. "And we're all praying for you."

Odd that in my bleakest moment, I felt God's love like never before. As we got in the car to go visit Ocieanna, it occurred to me that in Christ's darkest moment his love showed the most too. Love creeps into darkness—springs out of darkness. How odd is Christianity. And how loving and real is a Father who understands what we need.

We piled in our messy green van, and as I turned the key, Christian called out, "Papa! I forgot to say good-bye to Joe." Joe was Christian's best friend. "He's right there."

Joe ran toward the car. "Christian!"

"Go ahead, bud," I said and opened the van door.

Christian jumped out, and Joe hugged him. "I'm praying for your mom."

Christian hesitated, his scruffy hair tossed by the slight wind. "Thanks, Joe."

He climbed back into the van, and we drove away toward the hospital.

A few hours later, as the kids and I inched down the empty hotel-like hall toward Ocieanna's new room in the ICU, I set my mind to walk with confidence. To show the kids a strong Papa who trusted Jesus and possessed strength to face anything.

That was my goal, but limping on my broken ankle broke the façade. My stumbling mirrored the weakness only too evident inside. Then, a thought, like the butterfly in Abigail's picture, fluttered through my mind. Maybe it was okay for my children to glimpse my frailty. Maybe rather than a "strong Christian father," they could see me—just me—running to *my* Father in this scary place. Like I hoped they would.

Gabrielle's church shoes clicked rhythmically on the hard floor, but she didn't say anything, simply clung to my arm. Irritation, surely sparked from fear, tightened her jaw, as she seemed to forcefully clamp out the sight of her young sister, Abigail who giggled as she skipped along.

"Where's Mama at?" Abigail asked.

Ben's eyes focused on the door to Ocieanna's room. "The nurse said it's up ahead. Here, hold my hand."

Abigail slipped her little hand into her big brother's.

"I can't wait to see Mama." Christian stomped eagerly.

My two little ones exuded a confidence that if they could see their mom—cuddle her, smile at her—everything would be okay. They longed for her love, but I think they also longed to love her, to take care of her. It reminded me of how they delighted in bringing her flowers when she had a cold. *Surely our sweetness will make you better*, they seemed to say.

They would be disappointed this time. Their jubilant presence wouldn't ignite joyful light in her eyes. The dark coma prevented her—like a high, unclimbable stone wall—from hearing their kid voices, from receiving their tender offerings. Frustration gripped my gut. To see them disappointed, how I dreaded this. These thoughts hurt. I had to stop thinking.

Reaching the door, I squatted down to talk to them. "Guys, Mama looks a lot different. She won't be able to talk to you, okay?"

Abigail fingered her picture, her forehead scrunched. "I can hug her, though, right?"

"She can't talk?" Christian asked before I could answer Abigail. "Why not?"

"She's in a coma." Gabrielle rolled her eyes.

I felt my breathing quicken, so for a tiny moment I stared out a window at the trees swaying in the January bleakness. The clouds bulged heavy with a storm, but only the usual Seattle drizzle fell. I inhaled, put my hands on Christian and Gabrielle's shoulders, and then eyed Christian.

"Mama can't talk because she's asleep. She can't wake up, even though I know she would want to see you guys." Then I shifted to my Abigail. "You can hug her, sweetie, but she won't be able to hug you back."

Her lips slipped into a hesitant smile. "That's okay. I'll still hug her."

Ben grasped Abigail's hand again, and I wrapped my arm around Gabrielle as I opened the door.

As we slipped into the room a heaviness slowed our steps. Barely inside, the kids hesitated, each one gazing at Ocieanna from a distance. *Is this our mama?* their eyes seemed to say, even Ben's.

Slowly they took in the sight of their mama covered with tubes, surrounded by machines, with her half-closed eyes. Fear rolled over their faces like the looming shadow of a storm cloud. Christian's exuberance deflated. Abigail's joy disappeared. Tears flooded Gabrielle's cheeks. Ben's eyes also dampened with tears.

I moved to the front. "It's okay, guys. C'mon. Come see Mama."

I hoisted Abigail into my arms and guided Christian. As we reached near enough to touch her, Christian simply slid his hand into Ocieanna's.

He immediately gaped at me. "She's cold."

"Yes."

"They should warm her up." He rubbed her hand to heat it, and I let him.

Gabrielle sobbed quietly as she rested her messy brunette head against Ocieanna's chest. "Oh, Mama." She curled her fingers into Ocieanna's nightgown. "Please come back. Please." Her words were barely audible.

Ben leaned beside the head of her bed, his fingers softly stroking her hair.

"Mama," Abigail whispered, her eyes revealing the remnants of hope. "I made this for you." She held the butterfly picture in front of Ocieanna's face, then rested it on her chest. "I love you."

The whir of the breathing machine was the only response.

A frown pinched Abigail's lips. Her eyes drooped. "Papa?"

Kissing her head, I moved the picture to the bed stand. "It'll be right here when she wakes up."

"If ..." Gabrielle muttered.

Lord, let her wake up.

The little ones carefully climbed on the bed, avoiding the tubes, and Ben, Gabrielle, and I pulled chairs as close to Ocieanna as we could, our knees bumping the starched white sheet, our hands constantly touching each other.

"Ocieanna, I know you wouldn't want to miss church," I said.

"You love church." Christian leaned his head against her.

"So we'll read the Bible to you, okay?" Clinging to the only thing I knew, I opened the Bible app on my iPhone and read to her from Psalm 23.

We sang "Great is Thy Faithfulness," "Be Thou My Vision," and "Whate'er My God Ordains is Right," without a care about who heard us or how off-key we sounded. For over an hour, we lingered, clinging to those moments, longing, begging for our dear mama to wake up.

The sky outside the window darkened, and soon Ocieanna's friend Rosalyn arrived. She was from the homeschool co-op and had offered to take the kids for the night. I spotted the shock on her face when she saw Ocieanna contorted by the tubes. Then compassion took over, and her blue eyes rounded. Her thin frame enfolded each of the kids in a hug. She prayed with us, even sang with us—another of God's people showering his presence over our broken hearts.

After we finished, she twisted toward the kids. "Do you guys want to go to my house?"

They looked at me, doubtful.

Part of me ached to keep them close. We were a family, we needed each other, and they tied me to Ocieanna. But of course, they couldn't stay here in the hospital all night. It was best for them to rest, perhaps be distracted from this heaviness for a time. I kneeled as they circled around me. "Time to go, okay?"

Abigail clung to my hand as the others warily shuffled toward Rosalyn.

"C'mon." Rosalyn's eyes brightened. "Do you like hot chocolate? You can have as much as you want, and we'll play games."

The three older kids forced weak smiles, but Abigail wouldn't let me go. She tugged on my arm, pulling me to her level. "I don't want to go," she whispered, tears moistening her plump cheeks. "I want to be with Mama."

She might never see her mama again. I wrestled this evil thought away as I wrapped my arms around her. "You need to rest so you can see Mama tomorrow," I spoke gently into her hair. "Will you pray for her?"

She didn't speak, just nodded. I let her hug me as long as she wanted, then stood back as she and the others walked through the door.

Sudden solitude wracked me, and my thoughts immediately flew to when it was only Ocieanna and I, before kids. "It's just us," I whispered. I kissed her face, her forehead, touched her golden brown hair. "Come back to me, darlin'. We've been through so much. We can make it through this too." I couldn't stop touching her, aching to be near—as long as I could. And as I whispered my love to her, a tear ran down her cheek.

I was shocked. "Are you in there, honey? Do you want to come back? Oh, babe, come back."

Finally, I moved to the armchair, gray like everything else in the shadows of this room. Exhausted by emotion, I sank into a numb problem-solving mode. Night's fathomless darkness arrived quickly. I phoned family, updated the church, all the time praying for my wife to survive. But as doctors and nurses shifted in and out, a new concern layered onto the others. The hospital staff warned me that if she survived, brain damage would be severe.

"Her brain was without adequate oxygen for ten minutes," the nurse, Alexandra, reminded me while checking Ocieanna's vitals. "I've seen this before. Some end up with the mental capacity of a four-year-old. I heard the doctor say if she comes out of the coma, she has about a twenty percent chance of ever going home."

As the door clunked shut behind her, I lay back in the incredibly uncomfortable chair made for family members to supposedly sleep on. Her words pummeled my mind and heart. I gazed at Ocieanna, frozen in the same position she'd been in all day, her eyes empty, her mouth filled with the breathing tube that stifled her usually tender voice. "If only I could fix you, darlin'."

My organized mind thrust me forward to the worst-case scenario. I felt compelled to prepare for life as a widower—a single dad. Even if she survived, I'd still be on my own. The chances were so slim that she'd ever be the same Ocieanna again. But how could I prepare for something like that? I couldn't. The unknown stumbled me. Hope stumbled me. I didn't want to hope; honestly, I was afraid of being disappointed. Perhaps, as a good Christian, I should've embraced hope. But I didn't feel like a good Christian that night. I was a scared child who couldn't let go of Nurse Alexandra's words.

She might never wake up, but if she does …

Twenty percent, if she comes out of the coma … only twenty percent chance of a normal life.

Finally, sleep won out over my restless thoughts.

I don't know how long I slept when …

Ding! Ding! Ding!

Alarms woke me, along with the sound of several hospital workers rushing into the room. I glanced at the clock. 4:14. Adrenaline banishing any semblance of sleepiness, I shot to my feet. "What's happening?"

Ignoring me, a male nurse shouted, "She's arresting again!"

A woman began chest compressions. "Get the defibrillator!"

Chapter Four

SHADOW OF DEATH

You have fed them with the bread of tears
and given them tears to drink in full measure.
(Psalm 80:5)

"Please stand clear."

Is this really happening again?

The chaotic line on the screen. Ocieanna's heart not beating. The feminine mechanical voice.

"Push button."

Her body jolted. No reaction.

She's dead. Again! My Ocieanna. If I was afraid before, this fear now towered over, engulfed, eclipsed the previous offender. It controlled me. I couldn't move. Couldn't think. *She's dead. Really dead.*

Again, "Please stand clear."

Tears stung my eyes. I couldn't wrestle them back.

The nurses stayed focused on Ocieanna, working quickly, decisively.

"Push button."

The door clicked open and a sick patient's cry echoed from the hall. This distracted the male nurse at the helm. He hesitated.

"What are you doing?" A female nurse with a tight ponytail tore into him. "Push it!"

He did and Ocieanna again jerked, but I knew to concentrate on the monitor. Breath refused to fill my lungs, and I became lightheaded as I waited, thinking—knowing—the shock wouldn't restart Ocieanna's heart. How could she survive two cardiac arrests in two days? The fact that her pulse beat again after the first one blew away the odds. Could this happen twice? No. It couldn't possibly …

Again, no sign of life.

Panic escalated. *Oh God! She's going to die.* I screamed inside, aching to vent my horror but forcing myself to keep quiet, not divert the distractible nurse. Yet my mind wouldn't stop wailing in terrified sound bites. *I'm losing her. Oh God, please, please help!*

"Press button."

My eyes stayed peeled on the monitor—and then a weak rhythm appeared. A heartbeat.

"Oh my God," I said as I collapsed into the chair. I wasn't taking the Lord's name in vain. I never meant those words more in my life.

While the nurses stabilized Ocieanna, their faces troubled me. I perceived doubt, distance, like they didn't want to care, knowing she would … be gone soon.

As the chaos wound down and I slowly breathed again, the gloomy morning's sinister light snaked through the gray blinds. Quiet reigned—a fearful smothering silence. I stared at Ocieanna, remembering the tear on her cheek last night. Why? Why would God give me that hint of hope, only to dash it again?

When I was a child, my parents had taken me to the beach in Southern California. On one trip, I meandered out along a rocky pier and slipped. In a second the waves slammed me against jagged black rocks. Completely at the mercy of the waves, I flailed until a hand finally pulled me out.

I was that child again, hurled helplessly against deadly rocks.

In the midst of this turmoil, an older lady from church arrived. Elaine. She wore a sympathetic smile and a strong stature. She looked like she was ready for anything. Edging to my chair, she motioned to hug me, but I flinched. No. No hugs. Not now. She stepped back awkwardly.

"How's she doing?" Compassion ruled her face, but I couldn't receive it. The nurse, Alexandra, who had slid in at some point, answered, but I didn't listen.

As they spoke, I realized I had only one winning move. Shut down my emotions completely. The last two days, I had scrambled to balance them—allowed myself to feel some but not too much. That wasn't working. I needed to be numb. I had to stop feeling.

Ocieanna was going to die, no doubt about that. No more false hope. No more unrealistic expectations. She would be gone within days—hours? Preparing for this rose to first priority. What would the next days hold? I'd care for the kids, organize our new life, and one more thing—plan a funeral.

The only funeral I'd been involved in before was Ocieanna's mom's. The cancer battle had been long and painful. Her mom's death was the end of suffering for her and the beginning of ever-lasting joy. The funeral preparation—busy, even stressful at times—carried peace and joy and grace along with grief. My wife's funeral would not be like that.

I glanced down at my broken ankle and viewed it as an obstacle to my new role—single dad, funeral planner. Somehow I remembered it was Monday, and my surgery was scheduled for today—to remove the pins. Okay. Now I had a plan. I would go to that surgery. I would start my ankle mending. Get that done, so I could do the rest.

I focused on Elaine. "You're here to take me to the surgeon, get my pins taken out of my ankle?"

She nodded. "I'm the one who signed up."

My stomach ached, and something like anger simmered. I didn't want her with me. I could walk to the surgeon from here. I wasn't completely immobile. And having someone around was too risky. I had to focus. Compassion, empathy, tenderness—they were the last things I needed. I needed to be logical, emotionally cold.

I threw on a blue sweatshirt Ocieanna had tucked away in my car in case I needed it. "You really don't have to come with me. I can get myself there." I didn't mean to be rude, but I didn't care either.

Gazing at me unwaveringly, like a mom, she said, "You shouldn't be alone. Let's go." Her white hair quaked as she motioned toward the door.

Like a rebellious teenager, I snapped, "Fine."

Beneath darkening clouds and thickening raindrops, she drove me across the parking lot to the office where a doctor would slide out the steel pins that had held my tibia to my fibula for the last three months. I stayed silent, not bothering to politely make conversation. Instead, I fixated on the task at hand; once the pins were out, I'd be stronger. Ready.

I brushed rain from my sleeve as we entered the blue-tinged waiting room where I signed in at the front desk. I felt my chin quiver as I spoke. Speaking—even about insignificant things—threatened to break the dam.

I found a seat in the row of navy blue vinyl chairs near the bank of windows. The wind hammered outside, behind me. A mother sat with her young boy whose arm was in a bright green cast. A few years ago, Ben had broken his arm by falling out of a tree at church. I wondered what had happened to this boy. A toddler climbed over the seats, and the mother also held a baby, trying to feed it from a baby food jar. Messy. She appeared frazzled, and I felt sorry for her. But jealous too, not of her but of her husband.

Soon I would be among those men who raised children alone.

I would be alone. My chest ached, physically, as if someone were relentlessly punching me.

The image of Ocieanna arresting the second time replayed over in my mind. I fought to banish it, but the more I strove, the stronger the memory came back.

Her face had turned blue again.

Her body so limp, powerless.

Her hands—I kept seeing her hands—not moving, as if numb. As if dead.

Oh, God, I can't do this anymore.

And I lost it. My neck became rubber. My head fell into my hands. I wept. Right there in the waiting room. Great, heaving sobs from the depths of my lungs, my gut—my soul.

"His wife's in the ICU. She just had a heart attack," I heard Elaine say—to whom, I didn't know. She put her hand on my back, but I stiffened, so she removed it.

It wasn't a heart attack, where a blockage can often be treated. Cardiac arrest. Ocieanna's heart suddenly stopped for no reason. Didn't Elaine know that? Cardiac arrest seemed so much worse.

The receptionist walked over to me. "Do you want us to reschedule this? We don't have to remove the pins today."

I shook my head, still heaving sobs.

"He wants to do it today," Elaine offered.

Almost simultaneously, the nurse came out from the back and called my name. I rose and shakily limped after her, still unable to stifle the fear and sadness constricting my shoulders. A few moments later, as I faded beneath the anesthesia haze, one thought pierced my mind. When I awoke, would I be a widower?

Part Two

OCIEANNA'S STORY

Chapter Five

MY FATHER

For the Father himself loves you.
(John 16:27)

My journey to life—to love like there's no tomorrow—began before I woke up. I don't know why the Lord included this chapter as a prologue to all I would learn in the coming months and years, but I'm grateful he did. While still in the coma, I found myself confronted with a beautiful, surprising encounter with my deceased father. A vivid dream of him and me.

Much of my struggle to receive love from anyone really, especially God, stemmed from my dehydrated, debilitated relationship with this man.

Even though I had three siblings, I was my dad's only child. Mom had been married twice before, so my sisters and brother were his stepchildren. Dad favored me over the others—in a sick, needy way. When a young child, I delighted in his overattentive love, but it soon became a treacherous burden—a wall separating me from my siblings and even my mom. She once told me she didn't need to parent me because I "had my dad." How I longed for her love. And the love of my siblings too.

How I resented my dad for stealing them from me.

But this chasm wasn't the only effect his unhealthy "love" caused. When a parent depends on a child for his own self-esteem, when he shames the child for expressing emotion or becomes enmeshed with the child, neglecting healthy boundaries, this, I've learned, is a type of abandonment.

In me, it bred resentment.

By the time I reached junior high, an icy wall separated my heart from Dad's.

On one occasion, a whole childhood of frustration, anger, and, in some ways, even disgust toward my father rose to its boiling point. It was about bowling of all things.

From the time I was about seven, my father had enrolled me in a Saturday kids' bowling league. I bowled while he kept score. I wanted to quit for years, not because I didn't like bowling but because he criticized me relentlessly, adding to my bitterness toward him. But I knew quitting would hurt his feelings. I was still young, and guilt won out, so I kept bowling.

Years went by. I bowled. I resented him. I bowled some more. Finally, on a roasting-hot Saturday morning in the Southern California desert, compassion ran dry. As a fourteen-year-old Christian teen, I loved my heavenly Father, and knew I should love my earthly father too, but I wasn't there yet. Stone barricades, erected by years of disappointment, fortressed my heart. I didn't trust him, care what he thought, or even like him.

My over-sixty-year-old father and I piled into his recently bought gold sedan and trekked from our fancy gated community along the dry tumbleweed fields toward Sun City Bowl. It was the last week of the bowling session. An air-conditioned wind filtered its antifreeze smell through the front seats. I stared straight ahead.

"I don't want to sign up again," I said, bracing myself, ready to withstand his piteous pleas.

"You … what?" Tilting his gray-haired head toward me, the wrinkles under his eyes drooped. "Why?"

Tired of his weak guilt trips, I folded my arms and rolled my eyes. "I don't want to."

"It's our time together …" He deluded himself into thinking we were together. I existed so far from him—always.

"I just don't want to." Hurt anger walled in my heart. I'd had this fight in my head a million times. I wouldn't be fooled into feeling sorry for him. I'd had enough of that.

Despite his tall, stately demeanor, his bottom lip pouted, like he would cry, like not bowling with me represented the greatest fear of his life.

Disgusted by his weakness, I tightened my crossed arms. Why couldn't he say something like a real dad? *Okay, honey. You're a teenager now. It's probably time to move on from bowling.* Or, *Sure. Find something else you want to be involved in and I'll be your biggest cheerleader.* Or even better, *Let's pray together about what activities will build character in you and be fun.* I dreamed of this imaginary father.

Sadly incapable of these offerings, instead he pouted. "Don't you want to be with me?"

This final display of weakness pushed a button. In that moment, a fervent rile rose up. I refused to listen to his simpering. I wouldn't. He would not use me as his personal meaning for life. Not anymore. My hands trembled. My teeth clenched together until my jaw ached. And years of unexpressed frustration over my empty father-well thrust to the top. I couldn't hold my words back.

"I'm not going to bowl!" I yelled.

Shocked, he gripped the steering wheel with wrinkled hands, and he said what he always said when I openly expressed the slightest raw emotion. "Don't you talk to me like that!"

I slammed back in my seat, too frustrated to talk.

His fearful look reemerged. "Ocie, I love you so much. I …"

This triggered a scream from the depths of my emptiness. "You don't love me!"

Again, his face conveyed complete astonishment. "How can you say that? I love you more than anything. My whole life is loving you!"

Angry, confused, frustrated tears streaked my cheeks. "You only love me for *you*! You only love me for *you*! You only love me for *you*!" I kept screaming this phrase until my voice grew hoarse.

I honestly don't remember whether I signed up for bowling again or not. But for the rest of the drive, a stifling thick silence prevailed. No more talking, barely breathing. For the first time, I understood that his love repulsed me because it wasn't love. It was greedy, gluttonous need. I didn't have those words then.

After years of sinking in the muddy guilt of knowing he "loved" me too much, of striving to be the perfect child he idolized me as, of holding back my raw emotions in order to please him, I finally truly ingested that he shouldn't come running to me when he hurt, craving my smile of approval. A child should never exist only to make a parent happy. I was supposed to run to him. His duty was to lavish love on me, not to desperately replenish his own void, but freely, unconditionally. When he reversed those roles—as he did every day of my life—he stole my childhood.

After the bowling incident, I didn't think of him as a father anymore. Purely a man I had to tolerate. My love was cold. I broke that commandment, the one about honoring your father. Actually, I broke a few. Love your enemies. Humble yourself …

Yet, as I moved through high school, I fell more in love with Christ. I didn't want to sin against my dad anymore. For Christ's sake—because I loved him—I tried to love my dad. I sought to accept his meager, unsatisfying love and find the rest of my fathering in Jesus. As a result, I purposed to be loving, to offer him at least a portion of the attention he thirsted for. I failed at this, a lot. But I tried.

Then, when I was a junior in high school, one evening as I lounged on the couch in our comfortable house, eternity broke into our living room. Dad sat next to me. The old defensiveness rose, just at his presence, but I recovered myself and offered a smile.

After a few moments of awkward silence, he patted my knee. "Ocie, what does it mean to be a Christian?"

My breath wedged in my lungs. Was he really asking me this? He rarely spoke about "religion." Forced to go to church as a child, he'd discarded faith as an adult.

He moved his aging hands to mine as I shared the simple gospel.

"We are all sinners," I said.

His forehead creased. "I thought sinners were really bad people, punks, hoodlums."

"No, Dad. We all sin."

A glimpse of acknowledgment.

"Jesus died so our sins can be forgiven. If we trust in him, we will be accepted by the Father."

He angled his head. "What do I have to do?"

"Nothing. Just believe."

His shoulders relaxed, like at that moment Jesus had lifted his burden. His eyes smiled, lovingly, genuinely—a look I didn't recognize. A new look.

"Do you believe this?" I asked, my voice shaky—my soul doubting God could change my father's heart.

His head hung low, but he raised his eyes to meet mine. "Yes, I do."

A sword of hot joy pierced my heart. An urge to fall on my face before God infused me. *Forgive me for my doubts. Forgive me for not loving him the way you do. Thank you. Thank you, Jesus, for answering my prayers, for saving my father.*

Together in our cozy rust-colored living room, I prayed the sinner's prayer with my dad.

Awe and joy filled my heart. My father found in God the love and forgiveness I struggled so terribly to give him.

For a long time, Dad appeared to be a Christian, but ten years later, after my mom died, he stopped going to church or reading his Bible. And he became even more emotionally demanding of me than when I was a child (if that's possible)—calling me incessantly, exaggerating his health issues, lying about his needs. Again, I felt sorry for him and gave in to his demands.

But like when I was a child, this selfish "love" exhausted me. Drained me. One cold February afternoon, it came to an explosive, emotional head—like the bowling scene, with tears, screaming, and especially heartbreak.

Just when I nearly shut him out completely, Michael and I transferred to Los Angeles for his work. Relieved, I prayed the distance would bring healing and that Dad would stop putting his hope in me, instead placing it in the only one who could fill his yawning love void.

Moving day arrived. Michael had already gone to California while I finished up the details. My apartment sat empty, stark. The gray carpet against gray walls mimicked the gray Seattle weather outside. Gray, gray, gray—just like I felt inside. Everything was ready to go. I would've felt confident, excited for a new adventure, but my father, who had insisted on overseeing the final packing, roiled in a tight wad of nerves.

His anxiety spread over me like a tarp of darkness as I consolidated the final few boxes onto the tile next to the front door.

Hovering nearby, he asked, "Did you get your deposit back?" He didn't wait for a response. "I saw Michael didn't fix the drain in the shower. You won't get your deposit if it's not done."

This, merely one of a torrent of criticisms, clogged me like the drain.

My stomach ached. I longed to flee, to get away from his prison of gloominess. Yet what kind of daughter would run from her father? What had he really done except drown me in negativity and stalkerlike "love"? I should extend grace. After all, he was a Christian—my brother as well as my father.

This thought became the spindly thread that kept me going. *He's a Christian. He's in God's hands. I don't have to fix him. God will.*

But as he continued nagging, complaining, and criticizing, a terrifying doubt niggled its way. *What if he's not a believer? Worse, what if he's been faking it all these years?* This terrified me because if he lied to me about that, it would feel like the greatest betrayal of my life. I could deal with him simply not following Christ, but to lie in some historic attempt to win my sympathy? It was unthinkable.

Without a clue as to what he was saying, I blurted out, "Dad, will you keep going to church after we leave?" I held my breath.

He shrugged his shoulders, like a teenager.

All the mounting rage was ignited by that shoulder shrug. For the first time since the bowling incident, I screamed at him. "You won't, will you? Why? Why would you lie to me?" All the other hurts rushed to the surface. "And why are you even here? I can pack my own house! I don't need you to tell me to get my deposit back! I'm not a child!"

The dank living room blurred in my view as rage invaded my vision. Dad stumbled backward, as if struck.

"You've got to stop finding your happiness in me. You are a Christian, Dad. You should find joy in Christ. You need to read your Bible. Pray. Want to serve others. Go to church." My hands shook. Unreleased sobs battered me. "Are you even a Christian?" I folded my face in my hands, weeping, in a way relieved to have aired this out, but mostly frustrated that I couldn't find a better way to get through to him. I wasn't fourteen anymore. I knew better than to berate my father. I loved him. I longed for a good relationship.

Dad took a step closer to me. I expected him to defend himself, but strangely, it was like the father gene suddenly activated and he morphed into a real father. With both hands, he gently trailed his fingers over my long hair. "Ocie," he said, his voice soft. "You don't have to worry about me. Of course I love Jesus. Of course I'll go to church." He dropped his wrinkled hand to hold mine, and I stiffened at his warm touch. "I promise." For the first time in my life, he wiped my tears.

How I longed for this moment to be real, but I couldn't trust it. Was this my true father, hidden all those years from me, or just another manipulation? Another way for him to play with my emotions, win me over. *This is your last chance*, I thought, intentionally, almost out loud.

I cautiously let him hold me, hoping desperately that he would keep his promise, but doubting he would.

One sunny morning, two months later, in my kitchen in California, on the phone, I asked him if he had been going to church.

He said no.

My hands trembled as I realized this was the beginning of the end of our relationship. Not because I judged him for not going to church, but because he had broken his promise. I couldn't know if the foundation I'd based our relationship on—that he'd become a Christian when I was sixteen—was true.

Not surprised by his answer, I remained calm. I didn't rebuke him. I didn't get angry or try to convince him. I just whispered, "You promised," almost to myself.

He chuckled nervously and gave an excuse.

After I hung up, emotion exploded and I yelled absurdly at the cat. I sobbed over my dad, hard. But for the last time.

After that, I finally accepted reality. My father would never love me how I wanted. His father had abandoned him as a child, his mother was strict, cold. He simply didn't have the capacity to love me.

I understood this, but at the same time I had to shield myself and my family—had to construct protective, not bitter, walls. From then on, we had little more than a superficial relationship. He completely distanced himself from his faith. Disappointment scraped my heart as I fought to rest in my heavenly Father's care.

A day before he died (from complications of Parkinson's), in his hospital room, he beamed when I approached his bed—his deathbed. "Ocie. You're here!" As I settled down next to him, he studied me expectantly, as if still desiring my approval. Then he cautiously cupped my face in his frail, aging hand.

Moved by compassion, I hugged him, kissed his smooth, age-spotted forehead, and then, like an unforeseen rainstorm, the deep-rooted longing for a father's love overtook me. But too much heartache seeped through every thought of him. Even then, I dared not hope for a pure, unselfish love. My walled heart shut out any feeling of love for him. I felt compassion, though, and fear for his soul.

Apparently he feared too. He asked, "Will you read the Bible to me?"

So I moved to the stiff chair and read Psalm 23.

Did his cracked and parched soil receive God's Word? I couldn't know. But I prayed it did.

Even after his death, my relationship with Dad never felt resolved. Memories of him brought pain, not joy.

And then I saw him, nine years after his death, in a lifelike coma dream.

Now I was the one in a hospital bed, but mine was draped with snow-white sheets in a meadow bordered by mighty evergreens. The grass sparkled brightly, like when morning's first dew frolics with fresh sunbeams. As golden flowers peeked out among the bushes along the tree line, the sun shone from a blue-beyond-this-earth sky.

I shifted my head to the side and saw him. My tall, stately father, not acting stately but joyful—youthful. His face glowed with a huge grin, the smile I longed for as a child but rarely received. His arms flung open, as if welcoming me into an embrace. Again, so not like him. As he paced toward me, his gaze caught mine with kind, loving eyes.

Loving. Real love emanated from his eyes, not the fake, selfish, empty "love" he had always offered me. I don't know for sure, but maybe this dream was to show me that Dad finally found the love he so longed for—in heaven. And maybe that heavenly love transformed him. Love can do that.

And maybe my journey would begin with a step toward freeing my father memories from the burbling caldron where they still oozed. I gradually realized, am still realizing, that forgiveness doesn't snap into action all at once, but slowly. As we walk with a forgiving Savior, we become like him.

From that point on, without pretending my father's neglect—or the other scarring events—didn't happen, perhaps I could embrace a new calling. Could my death have been to overcome my childhood-born perfectionism, insecurity, and self-loathing in order to receive love, abide in it, and shower it on everyone I could? Truly that would be worth dying for.

Maybe this was the beginning of loving like there was no tomorrow.

Daddy! my heart cried out to the daddy I'd always craved—the happy, open, confident one I fantasized about, right there embedded in my own father. My father but different. New. Transformed by love.

One last moment of precious, loving eye contact, then … a voice pulled me away.

Chapter Six

SEARCHING
FOR MICHAEL

Arise, my love, my beautiful one, and come away.
(Song of Solomon 2:10)

"Cieanna."

A voice floated to me, a woman's, loving, gentle.

Dad was gone, the dream too, and now slanted light struck my vision. Shaded shapes took form as I sailed toward consciousness. Arising from a coma differed from waking from a night's sleep.

I glided along a silent, mysterious river, not feeling anything, only emptiness. Then the river forked, and I angled toward a familiar stream. A homeward stream. Awe-filled joy replaced the blankness.

My senses switched on, vaguely independent of each other, whirling around me as I delighted in the vortex. *Someone's touching my hand—isn't that wonderful? I think those shady forms are people. How lovely! I hear a voice, a nice voice.*

Eventually, my senses slowed their spiral, and I began to relate to the outside world normally, yet still basking in wonder. Consciousness itself was a delicious, magical gift.

I became more aware of a cool hand holding mine, and then a

different woman's voice ruptured through—rougher than the one before but still kind.

"Ocie, we're here." This one tugged at memories from long ago. She called me Ocie. Only people from my childhood knew me as Ocie, not Ocieanna. Yet why would the soft, sweet voice I heard first be joined with this person from my past?

I fixated on this odd combination of voices. I didn't anxiously wonder where I was, or why I'd been asleep, or why I was attached to machines. I couldn't figure out why these two people had converged in my presence.

When I focused on the faces, I grew even more confused.

The soft, loving tone belonged to my friend Kim. Oh, how I loved seeing her round cheeks perked in a smile. Her flowing white hair and perfect makeup bespoke her usual elegance, but her dimpled smile carried an endearing goofiness I cherished. She lived in my church world, the circle of Christian brothers and sisters with whom I journeyed down the narrow path.

The other face belonged to my sister-in-law, Tonya, a down-to-earth woman with straight blond hair and wide nonrimmed glasses. She had a raspy voice, tattoos, and a bellybutton ring. Compassionate and caring, she'd be there for anyone in need without hesitation. A newer believer.

Both faces smiled at me sympathetically, like mothers ready to comfort a sick child. They also inspected me, apprehensively searching for clues—of what I didn't know. Their shoulders were stuck in a raised position, their elbows fixed stiffly to their sides.

What would bring these two into the same room? What made them sit by my bedside staring at me with hopeful yet concerned eyes? Tears moistened their cheeks. The only thing they had in common was me. They loved me.

Manners took over. All I could think to do was introduce these two women from different worlds.

"Kim, have you met Tonya?" My first words after waking up from death, from a drug-induced coma.

Both of their shoulders relaxed. Kim exhaled. "Yes, Ocieanna, we've met." She chuckled nervously, almost giddily.

Immense delight spread across Tonya's face. "We're glad you're here." She patted my arm, then threw a glance toward someone standing behind her. A nurse. She also wore a huge, almost silly grin.

I didn't know why Tonya said she was glad I was here, and I definitely didn't get what the goofy smiles were about, but I didn't think Tonya realized that she and Kim didn't know each other. I *had* to fix that.

"Tonya, have you met my friend Kim?"

They assured me that they had met each other.

"We're so glad you recognize us." Kim was practically bouncing in her seat. I thought she might let out a "Yippie skippy!" like she does sometimes.

"And you're talking," Tonya added with glee.

As I settled into this new concept of being awake, I realized that as oddly blissful as I felt, I wanted something. I ached for someone. So once I got over repeatedly introducing Kim to Tonya and Tonya to Kim, my gaze sought him out.

My giddy visitors must've seen my eyes shift because they moved aside—in slow motion it seemed, like clouds parting—to reveal him. My Michael, gazing at me with love in his deep-brown eyes. Oh, that love-like-no-tomorrow love. His gaze embraced me like a homespun quilt, like a long-lost sweetheart, like heaven's love.

His brown-black hair flopped messily as he crossed the room to me, touched my cheek, gently kissed my forehead, my lips. Everything in me perked toward his presence, like flowers seeking the sun. Finding his place next to the head of my bed, he wrapped his arm around my shoulder, warming it with his gentle yet strong protection.

"Hey, darlin'."

His voice. Of all the sensory experiences I'd enjoyed over the last few minutes, his voice incited the richest, most delighted response from my fuzzy brain to my awe-filled soul. His voice brought an ocean of familiar comfort and peace. It spoke acceptance, safety, inclusion. His voice carried me home.

"Michael Fleiss," I whispered, still dazed as I nestled my head against his upper arm. "You're here."

He didn't speak. Joyful emotion stifled his words. Kissing my forehead again, he wet it with silent tears.

As the guests filtered to their homes, Michael delicately recounted what happened. "You had a cardiac arrest."

I lifted my hand to my chest. "My heart? But my heart's fine. Why?"

"They don't know. It just"—his voice cracked and he swallowed to clear it—"stopped."

"Stopped?" My stomach fluttered as my brain worked to comprehend. "My heart stopped? So, I … Honey, you're saying I—"

Michael nodded, smoothed my hair. "I almost lost you, darlin'."

I tugged him closer and nestled against him. I knew, somehow, what he said was true. But at the same time, it couldn't be. I died? My heart stopped? That was too outrageous. I closed my eyes. Inhaled his presence.

Michael continued, "Paramedics brought you here."

Again, not me. I was young. Only forty-two. I had kids to take care of. I was a busy lady. Healthy. I thought of ambulances sirening down the street, tried to imagine myself in one. Then it hit me. If the paramedics came, maybe our EMT friend Jay was one of them.

"Did Jay come?"

Not knowing the direction my thoughts had come from, Michael looked surprised. "Um, no honey. Jay didn't come."

Staring at Michael, I realized it wasn't surprise but amusement prancing in his eyes. "Did I ask that already?"

His eyes glinted, amused. I'd apparently asked it several times. He clarified (for the third time) that I would struggle with short-term memory loss as my brain recovered. With time my memory would improve, but they didn't know how long it would take. This resonated as true too. Memories glossed along in vagueness, as if the thoughts parading through my mind were only dreams. Except for a few things. Michael. The kids. I remembered them, wanted them.

"The nurses are excited you can talk at all." Wonder tinged his voice. "They were concerned before you woke up. Most people who survive a cardiac arrest can barely function."

"Brain damage?"

"Yeah."

"But not me?"

He shook his head. "You're doing great. They—the nurses—say it's a miracle. They've never seen anything like it."

"Really?" A humbled sob clutched my throat, threatening to release into tears.

I played with his fingers, held them to my cheek, kissed his palm. "And I'm okay now?" I was okay. I knew.

He smiled weakly. He wasn't as sure as I, but that didn't scare me. Nothing but peace and love embraced me. And something else—a desire. Glancing out the window at the city lights decorating the night sky, I hungered to experience the world again. Life, not some grand new adventure.

I wasn't craving traveling the continents or skydiving. I simply wanted *my* life. My simple, love-filled world. Michael, my kids, our church, the house, my friends. The world where I still dwelt had somehow transformed to a glorious beauty, and I wondered why God had brought me back to my life. Was there a bigger reason?

I'd asked this question before. This wasn't the first time I nearly lost my life.

"Daddy, Becko flew out the window!" My three-year-old heart thumped. Tears warmed my face. How would my imaginary friend Becko survive jumping from an airplane way up in the sky? And why did he do it? Was he scared like me?

My dad glowered at me, took a breath, and then his bushy brown eyebrows pouted. He was afraid for Becko too. I wondered if he would tell the pilot, who had given me wings when we boarded, to stop the plane. I mean, we couldn't let Becko die.

Dad stretched his tall top half over me to look out the window. He smelled like the white stuff he put all over his face every morning.

"I can see him," he assured me. "Don't worry. Becko can fly. He'll meet us in Portland."

No way. "Becko can fly?"

"Yep." He seemed convinced.

"But how come I never saw him do it before?"

Dad sighed. I think my questions frustrated him. "Maybe he only flies when he's on an airplane."

I could accept that. "But what if he goes back to Alaska?"

"He won't. I told him where we were going before we left."

Tears made my eyes sting.

Dad patted my leg and handed me Snowy, my bear. "Don't be unhappy, Ocie, please. How about I read you a book?"

I didn't want to make my dad sad too, so I said okay, even though I still worried about Becko. I cuddled Snowy as Dad read to me.

A few hours later, Dad, Mom, Snowy, and I landed in Portland. Becko was there waiting for me. He came with us to the hospital.

A nurse with long blond hair walked us to a yellow-painted room. "This is where you will stay," she said brightly. I wasn't used to grown-ups talking to me directly, but I liked the attention.

My mom's eyebrows bunched up. Her hair—all poofed up on top of her head as usual—looked messy. Strands naughtily wandered away from the rest. I think Mom was mad. She didn't like being there. It was a bother to be there. I bothered her a lot even though I tried not to.

"Why are there bars on the bed?" I asked the nurse.

My mom frowned.

I'd asked a dumb question. I did that a lot too.

"We don't want you falling out of the bed." The nurse chuckled. I didn't know why, but it made me feel bad. I laughed along anyway.

"Will the doctor be here soon?" Mom asked.

As they talked, my stomach got achy. I had to go potty, but I was afraid. It burned when I tinkled. I didn't want to go. I started to cry.

"Oh, honey." The nurse knelt down in front of me. "What's wrong?"

I hugged my mom's leg and hid my face, crossed my legs.

"Do you have to go potty, Ocie?" Mom's voice, always so firm.

The nurse handed me a cup to pee in, then pointed me to the bathroom just outside the door. "I'm sorry it hurts you, honey. That's why you're here. To get you all fixed up so it doesn't hurt anymore."

I was glad I had Becko and Snowy.

My kidney—the left one—didn't work, I was told. It was making my insides yucky, like if a sewer backs up. It's why I felt sick and weak.

After two days of being poked with sharp needles, having cold metal things stuck on me, and talking to doctors who didn't really see me, a group of doctors and nurses came into my room. They spoke in serious voices, words I didn't know.

Then they gave me clean jammies. Real stiff ones that didn't fit very well.

They laid me on a bed that had wheels and rolled me down the hallway. It squeaked as it rolled against the flat-tiled floor. Mom and Dad walked with me, holding my hands. I shivered from the cold, and Dad said things like, "Don't worry," and "You're going to do great." His forehead didn't look normal though. Eyebrows smushed together.

He told me I would go into a room, fall asleep, and then when I woke up he and Mom would be there, and I could have Kool-Aid. I liked Kool-Aid, and as long as Mom and Dad stayed with me …

We came to big metal swinging doors, and a person dressed all in white with a mask and hat came out. At first I couldn't tell if it was a boy or girl.

"I'm sorry, sir, madam. You can't go past this point." It was a man, and he didn't sound sorry. He sounded mean.

My parents let go of my hands.

Scared. Suddenly I was really scared, like when I thought I was going to drown at the pool.

I twisted in my bed-cart, the stiff pajamas scratching my skin. "You're not coming with me?"

Reaching for them, I cried. The mean guy in white kept pushing the squeaking cart. Why? Why was he doing this? I wanted my mommy and daddy. My hands felt cold without their touch.

"Mommy!" I cried as they pushed me through the doors.

"No! Daddy!" I sobbed as the man silently wheeled me into an ugly white room with a big light that blinded me. So cold, I shook as other white-dressed people worked around me. I couldn't see their hair or their mouths.

The mean guy put a mask over my nose and mouth and told me to count. I knew my numbers, so I counted. Then I started to choke. *I'm going to die.*

When I woke up, I didn't have my kidney anymore. I didn't feel it gone. That's just what they told me. My tummy really hurt, super bad. And it stung even more to go potty. They put a tube down there, and when the pee went through, I screamed and grabbed onto my mom.

She said, "Just do it, Ocie. Get it done."

When we boarded the plane to go home, Becko flew away again, even though I asked him not to. But he was there when we got home to Anchorage, Alaska.

Over the years I came to realize more about what it meant to have my kidney out. When I was about ten, my big sister Dawn visited. We had moved to California, and she, still a teen, had stayed in Alaska with her new husband and baby. While driving to lunch, she contemplated me for a moment, then blinked her fiery eyelashes.

Her staring made me squirm. "What?"

"It's amazing you survived."

I gawked back at her, confused.

"You were so young, Ocie, when they took out your kidney. Mom and Dad were freaked out. They thought you were going to die."

I stared at my hands.

"You're special. You must have some big purpose, y'know. Some reason why you didn't die."

Nausea gripped my stomach. Fear clenched my shoulders. I was an awkward girl. Bullied at school. My goal in life was to be invisible. To *not* stick out. Not to be "special."

I shrugged, and she moved on to other topics.

And now, cocooned in this hospital bed, relishing my breath, the pulse in my wrist, thoughts questioned. "Why Lord? Why did you save me?" Was I special? Did I have some purpose to fulfill? Was there some reason I survived death—twice?

I pondered the questions only briefly before an answer came.

No. I didn't think so. I hadn't been given some big purpose. I certainly wouldn't change the world. To be honest, I didn't even care about those types of things.

In that moment, I simply felt loved, embraced by God. Cherished as his beloved child. And that was all the answer I needed.

Chapter Seven

LONGING LOVE

For God is my witness,
how I yearn for you all with the
affection of Christ Jesus.
(Philippians 1:8)

*S*till in the hospital but out of ICU, I rested as Michael's lost-in-love face shone on me, encircling my heart with comforting acceptance like a feather bed. I'd journeyed a path without him—a dark, empty path. I longed for him. Just Michael. Not any role he played—not Michael my husband, Michael my kids' dad, Michael my counselor, my partner, my friend. I longed for him, his essence.

Now he was here, touching me, adoring me. Our union, almost wrenched asunder by "death do us part," had dodged a tragic ending. I clasped his hand, not cognitively aware of this truth but intensely feeling it.

Yet the circle wasn't complete.

"When can I see the kids?" I whispered. "How are they?"

I yearned for my kids. Not having them near left a gaping emptiness. My heart told me I was created to love those short people—and not emptying the love welling in me into their precious souls left me an abridged version of myself. To feel like me again, I *needed* to love them.

It reminded me of another time—a sad and lonely time—that birthed one of the happiest days of my life.

Before I had Ben, our oldest, I suffered through infertility for three years, culminating in two miscarriages. I'm not sure why, but sadly, my doctor wouldn't treat me until I lost *three* babies. So I had to wait, try to get pregnant, and then know the only way to receive care was to lose the baby.

Oh, the darkness of those days. Hopelessness and fear ruled my life. Every month I cried out in the spirit of the prophet Samuel's mother, Hannah, *Please grant me a child, Lord. Please heal what's wrong with my body so I can conceive. Don't forget me.*

At this time Michael received a grand promotion at work, transferring us from Washington State to the Pasadena, California, area. While there, a friend referred me to a fertility doctor.

Nervous pressure tensed my neck as I drove down Colorado Boulevard to the doctor's office. *Please let this work, Lord. Please.* I prayed, yet I didn't really think it would help. Fear had given way to cynicism.

Sitting on the chilly exam table, draped in a paper gown, I felt so vulnerable. Not just because of the invasive physical exam about to take place, but because this appointment represented the greatest pain in my life. I would trust this doctor, this man I'd never met, with my soul's fiercest craving—to hold a child in my arms.

He sauntered in, bringing a clean soapy smell. Tall, dark haired, handsome for an older man.

"Hello, I am Dr. Genho." His warmth and positive energy put me at ease. I liked him immediately. As we chatted, I discovered he was Lebanese—Michael's heritage. Something about that comforted me.

He performed a simple procedure, and within a couple of weeks the pregnancy test came out positive. Shocked and ecstatic, I immediately called Michael. Later, we snuggled together in our beautiful bedroom in our stylish new house and dreamed. But fear of another miscarriage always chafed the edges of my joy.

Tuesday morning, again my stomach churned as I drove down Colorado Boulevard to my appointment. Happy nerves, but fringed with fear, my emotions eddied like a gurgling stew.

Again, I lay on the exam table in the shaded room. Rather than just listening for a heartbeat, the doctor himself did an ultrasound to see if we could spy on the fragile life forming inside my womb.

I scrutinized a form of wobbling white against a black background. I had no clue what I was seeing, so instead, I fixed my complete attention on Dr. Genho. His dark-chestnut eyes concentrated beneath intense eyebrows. Then a glint leaked out—a bad glint. Worrisome.

My shoulders clenched up. My pulse sped, but I told myself to calm down. Maybe I was reading him wrong.

Relinquishing the ultrasound probe to the nurse, the amiable doctor tipped his squared jaw and took my hand in his. Dry, creased, but warm. "I'm sorry, Ocieanna . . ."

Immediately, moisture warmed my eyes. I sucked in air and held it to keep from hyperventilating.

"I don't see a heartbeat."

I withdrew my hand from his, thrust it to my chest. Not those words again. Three? Three of my babies dead. Why?

But before I could plunge too deep into despair, the doctor continued. "It's still very early. Come back in a week and we'll take another look." His lips nipped into a reassuring smile. "Don't worry." He patted my fisted-with-tension hand. "Okay?"

I nodded, acted like I would try not to worry, but that was a total façade. As soon as I spotted the hint of worry on his face, I spiraled into fear and anxiety. The rest of that Tuesday emptied into tearful despair. The next day, the same, but Thursday …

At a grocery store—Hughes, I think—I passed a display of grapefruit and my mouth literally watered. I'm not a big citrus fan. Barely ever eat oranges, and grapefruit even less. But I *had* to have one.

What a gift that craving was. As I delighted in what tasted like the yummiest grapefruit on the West Coast, my anxiety peeled away. I knew I was still pregnant.

I found out at the next week's appointment that I was right. I took Michael with me this time, and we had a quick party in the exam room when my darling baby's heartbeat raced. Dr. Genho even typed on the ultrasound "A strong heartbeat. Yippee!!!!!"

Soon after that, we moved back to Washington State. I often wonder if the whole reason for us moving to Pasadena that year was to meet the doctor who would help us finally become parents.

How I loved that baby in my belly. How I wanted him. Then after our Benjamin boy finally joined us, as I held him, touched his soft skin, breathed in that baby smell, I reveled in each moment. I'd doubted my arms would ever hold this tiny package, but I'd longed for him. My Jesus heard my cries, placing this precious gift in my care. The rocky path of loss that brought him to us ripened an intense love. Every moment spilled with magical, special … miraculous blessing.

Now, lying in ICU after dying twice, being a mommy to my four little loves again sparked this boundless thanksgiving in me, this supernatural mom love. Similar to that first desire to have a baby, a tangible longing for my children vanquished my heart.

I traced the curves of Michael's hand as he pondered my question about when the kids could visit.

His forehead creased. "I don't want them to wear you out, darlin.'"

Shadows darkened my heart, but I knew I should trust him, my wise protector, so I lifted a quick prayer. *Please let me see my babies soon, Lord.*

I palmed farther up his arm, relishing his nearness. "Maybe tomorrow?"

Michael must've seen the thirst in my eyes because he lifted my hand. Kissed it. "Tomorrow."

Hearing that, my fragile heart rested.

Chapter Eight

SISTERS

Above all, keep loving one another earnestly,
since love covers a multitude of sins.
(1 Peter 4:8)

est, the nourishing sanctuary of healing, lingered late into the next morning. As my eyes adjusted to waking, I was struck by yet another reason for awe and wonder. My two older sisters, Dawn and Jennifer, sat in chairs, muted against a milky natural light sifting through the long, narrow window. They had settled across from each other. Dawn's short red hair hung easily around her cheek as she read a magazine, thin knees tucked beneath her. Jennifer's athletic frame cozied into a chair as she fiddled with her phone, her black reading glasses sinking on her nose. They both emanated a peaceful beauty. I'd always thought they were so pretty, wished I could be like them.

My sisters, Lord. They're here.

Dawn must've heard my slight movement, because she shifted her gaze my direction. "Hey, Ocie." Her breathy voice rose to a smiling tone. "You're awake."

Jennifer pushed her glasses upward as she hooked her head toward me, her eyes moistening. "There you are."

Their presence bestowed my heart another boost of comfort. I hadn't seen them since my father's death nine years earlier. Nine years.

They moved to my bed, and Jennifer slipped her hand into mine, rubbed my arm.

"You're here." My voice cracked. It was almost unbelievable—this earthly reunion brought about by my death. I thought death only brought heavenly reunions.

Dawn slanted her head, joy emanating from her face. "You scared us." She cautiously patted my shoulder, then donned her oldest-sister authority. "You shouldn't do that!"

Jennifer burst into tears and awkwardly hugged me, her brown hair falling around my face. "I love you, Ocie."

Her faint scent of gardenia lotion brought memories. "I love you too, Jennifer. I love you."

We talked for a while, catching up about kids and jobs and relationships. Their voices sang dearly to me as they splintered open the doors of their lives. Yet how odd that sisters could live so separately and reunite with easy, flowing waves of love.

"Where'd Ocie go?" my father called out as he thresholded the house after working at March Air Force Base in Riverside, California.

Dust particles from the upholstered curtains tickled my nose while I, just a little six-year-old, waited behind them for my tall daddy's hand to swish away the fabric to find me.

"Where'd Ocie go?" He again pretended to seek me, while I unsuccessfully stifled giggles. "I need to find my girl."

I delighted in my father's searching for me.

Finally, after hunting under the couch cushions and behind the chair, he peeked behind the curtains and exclaimed, "There she is!"

"Daddy!" Overjoyed with my sneakiness, I hugged his long leg until he lifted me high in his arms.

How secure I felt. So happy—so trusting of his love.

And yet, something later soured this sweet memory.

When I was about fourteen, my mom and I were prepping spaghetti in the kitchen. She poured a spattering of Burgundy into the sauce from her wine glass, then her tidy short hair—a muted brunette at the time—shifted as she gulped her last sip and reached for the bottle. We talked about when I was a kid. That game I played with my dad popped to mind. I laughed as I reminded her of it.

"You know," she said, stirring the bubbling sauce, "while you and your dad played, Jennifer watched from the landing." She peered over her shoulder at me, eyebrows furrowed. "You knew that, didn't you?"

I stopped moving. A familiar ache struck my stomach. "What?"

She leaned against the counter. "I'll never forget the look on her face, like, *Why doesn't my daddy love me like he loves Ocie?* It broke my heart."

Guilt, rancid like sludge, dumped over me, transporting me back to the insecure, shamed child. One of the few pegs I could hold onto—that happy memory with my father—now morphed into another of many accusers.

I accepted full blame. Didn't even occur to me that it wasn't my fault my parents hadn't told Jennifer she was adopted by Dad. Seven years older than me, they could've walked her through it, loved her through it. That Dad *chose* to favor me—he could've fathered Jennifer with affection and generosity—also flew outside my surmising. He could've shown affection to us both instead of obsessing over me and neglecting her. Mom didn't have to tarnish my sweet childhood memory by revealing this sad story.

No. Their part of the blame wasn't even a possibility. Just my own guilt.

The guilt of knowing that because of me Jennifer believed her very own daddy loved her sister more than her. The stark emptiness

Jennifer must've felt as she perceived the most important man in her life choosing another, ignoring her. At least, this was how Mom saw Jennifer's lot, and I received this message of blame from her, added it to the stinking pile of unworthiness I'd been feeding myself for years.

Dad's favoritism didn't create a healthy environment for sisterly affection. Guilt kept me distanced from her. How could she love me when I stole her father away? I decided she didn't like me or want me around. Maybe she didn't. This could've been normal sibling conflict, but I believed Jennifer resented me. So I remained wary of her. I needed a friend, but it wouldn't be my sister.

Fortunately, as we grew to adulthood, a more mature understanding of childhood heartache and how it affects actions allowed me to move beyond the past bruises, let go of lingering bitterness. Sometimes, even as an adult, I longed for a sister-friend relationship, but we never grew close. We certainly didn't talk openly about our wounds (our family never did), but we employed an unspoken peace and mutual affection.

Separation defined my relationship with my oldest sister, Dawn, from the beginning.

I was five, still living in Alaska. A frosty chill from Mommy's hand penetrated through my pink knit glove as she gripped my wrist. We stood on the porch of Dawn's house. Mommy knocked, and we waited, quietly, very still.

No one came, and Mommy's jaw firmed up. "Darn it," she whispered, then knocked again.

I stared at the indented wooden squares on her door, then looked down to notice snow on my boots. I kicked it off. Dawn didn't live at our house anymore.

"Come in!" My sister's easy voice made its way to us.

Mommy opened the door and tugged me inside, but she didn't have to. I wanted to see Dawn, even though I knew Mommy was mad at her. We stepped into a cozy room with log walls, not white like the walls at my house. In front of a brown throw rug, a fire crackled. A wide bed sat at the far end of the room. *Does this house only have one room?* Dawn was propped up in it, her back against a latch-hook rug hanging on the wall. A handmade quilt was bunched around my sister's legs and waist. She held a tiny baby pressed to her chest.

A baby! Being the youngest sibling, babies awed and intimidated me, but mostly they sparked my curiosity. I let go of my mommy's hand and inched toward my sister. All I could see was the back of the tiny one's head, fuzzy with red wisps.

Dawn gave me a nice, warm smile. Her pretty red hair curled around her face. She looked different, happier, glowy. "Come meet your nephew, Jason."

I snuck forward, and she reached across the baby to hug me. My sister was almost as much of a mystery as the baby. Even though a big teenager, she spoke nice, looked at me when I talked, didn't make me feel stupid. But even when she lived at home, I didn't spend very much time with her. She was a faraway sister, so I hugged her tight until she let go.

Dawn adjusted Jason so I could see his face, all mushed up and wrinkly. I didn't know if he was cute. Were tiny babies cute? But he definitely appeared cuddly, even more than my bear, Snowy. I really wanted to hold him. I touched his cheek and gently palmed his silky fuzz.

"Where do you want these?" Mommy walked up behind me, arms filled with dirty clothes she'd picked up.

Dawn frowned, and a hurt hit my stomach.

"You don't have to do that, Mom," she said. "I'll get it when I'm done feeding Jason."

"I'm not sure why you have to breastfeed him. Bottles were good enough for me. My doctor said bottles were better."

Dawn jutted her jaw forward, like our dog Shane sometimes did before he barked. But Dawn didn't bark. She breathed in slowly. "What could be better for the baby than what my body provides?"

Mommy's eyes rolled and the side of her lip twisted up. "I'll just put these clothes in here." She plopped them in a laundry basket in a closet across the room.

I crawled onto the bed. Dawn placed the baby in my lap. Oh, he was so little. His skin so soft. So fragile. I was the most careful I could be with my itty-bitty nephew. My insides felt happy, in awe of this special thing, like a present, like Christmas.

I didn't understand why this neat gift made Mommy and Daddy so mad and sad. How? How could such a sweet little baby make them hate Dawn? I sure didn't hate her. I wanted to stay there all day so I could keep holding my baby nephew and be with my sister.

Mommy finally came over to the bedside. The baby's cuddliness seemed to make her feel happy too. She scooped him from my lap and held him. "Aren't you handsome," she said and kissed his head.

Dawn chuckled. "I think so."

"Me too," I said, but I didn't really think a baby could be handsome like a grown-up man.

I sighed, relieved that Mommy was happy again, but then she gave the baby back to Dawn and said we had to go.

I hugged my sister.

I don't remember seeing her again for many years.

Soon after Dawn became a mom, in her teens—still a child herself—we moved away from Alaska, leaving her to finish her youth on her own, with a baby.

Over the years, she'd visit us sometimes. I'd try to behave like I thought a sister should, but she was so much older.

Lonely, awkward, emotionally neglected child that I was, I truly longed for a sister like kids at school had, one to share secrets with, to hang out with, even to argue over the bathroom with. The sisters I knew felt at home with each other—but I didn't feel at home with anyone.

I admired Dawn, but from a distance. When she tried to talk to me, I answered awkwardly, fearful of saying something I shouldn't. Always afraid of doing something wrong, being stupid, a bother. Not because she dismissed me like that—she always showed me kindness—but I knew I wasn't like other kids. No comfortable sister relationship for me. So I floundered to figure out how I was supposed to act.

Interactions with Dawn left me unsatisfied. But even so, I loved her. An accepting realness in Dawn drew me, still draws me, to her. Also, her sadness, a lost-orphan wandering restlessness, caused me to wish love for her—and peace.

I don't know if I will ever be close to my faraway sisters, but on that day soon after my death, in our awkward unsettled way, we at least tried to be family.

"Okay, Ocie." Dawn zipped up her backpack as she scooted next to Jennifer, who stood by my bed holding my hand. "We're going to head out."

Jennifer enclosed my hand between hers. "We'll get together— all of us—in August, okay?"

I leaned my head against the pillow. "Yes, I would love that."

Dawn smoothed hair from my forehead. "It's a plan."

But we never got together. Years have gone by now, and I haven't seen them. Barely talked to my sisters.

That morning was yet another gift the cardiac arrest gave me. An island of togetherness in an ocean—a lifetime—of separation.

A moment to sweep aside the fog and reveal three broken, scarred siblings bonded by a past and blood that years may erode but not erase. And simply to remind me I have two sisters whom I love very much.

This thought wound its way into my soul, churning an inkling of another sibling relationship marked by separation. An older brother, my Jesus, whom I must also wait to see in the flesh, who one day will hold me in heaven. Yet, different than Dawn and Jennifer, even in the distance he's already closer than a brother and satisfies that sibling craving like no earthly one could.

> *One there is, above all others,*
> *Well deserves the name of friend;*
> *His is love beyond a brother's,*
> *Costly, free, and knows no end:*
> *They who once his kindness prove,*
> *Find it everlasting love!*
> *"A Friend that Sticketh Closer than a Brother"*
> —John Newton

Chapter Nine

I JUST WANTED *THEM*

But the LORD said to Samuel, "Do not look on his appearance
or on the height of his stature, because I have rejected him.
For the LORD sees not as man sees: man looks on the
outward appearance, but the LORD looks on the heart."
(1 Samuel 16:7)

From a reclined position—flat on your back in a hospital bed—you tend to focus on faces. I experienced lovely processions of affection each time I awoke from my many naps. On this morning, Tuesday, my friend Kim's smile blessed me, as did my sisters' and brother's. Their faces exuded love for me and relief that they still had me around.

On the third morning, my mind lingered in slight murkiness as I reveled in this new sense of feeling loved. I paused to truly appreciate the sincere affection combined with concern shining from the smiling faces around me.

As much as I cherished these dear folks, I continued to long for my kids. I still hadn't cast my gaze over their beautiful faces, or kissed their foreheads, or soaked in their childlike voices. Michael feared they would tire me, but I wondered if missing them drained me more.

Also, how odd to not be in charge of my little ones. I normally decided the elements of their day. I approved or rejected Abigail's outfits. I chose what to fix for breakfast, lunch, dinner, taking into account Ben's pickiness and Christian's appetite. As a homeschool mom, I determined whether Gabrielle would spend her morning on math or history. Now others bore those responsibilities, but it should've been me. I was the mom. No one else. My mommyhood stretched beyond my reach.

I chatted with my visitors, and Nurse Alexandra brought me a tray of rubbery eggs, cool bacon, and juice. As I munched, thoughts of my kids flickered nearby. In the midst of this, the door squeaked open.

So many people had come in and out that I should've been used to the sound, but each time the door opened, a flurry of hope tickled my belly. *Is it them?*

First, I spotted Michael's dark hair, but then he paused and placed his arm high up on the door, holding it open. Shifting my gaze lower, I felt an electric bliss course through me as another brown-haired head poked around.

I pushed the food tray aside as my boy Christian slinked closer, his brown eyes beaming with adoration. He didn't shriek with excitement, like when I arrived home from a trip, but his lips crooked in a smile. He meandered toward me, the others following.

"Hi, Mama," he whispered and gently, but without hesitation, climbed onto my bed and rested his head on my chest.

The others drew close to where they felt safest, attached to their mama, near, as tightly linked as they could get.

"I want to be next to Mama." Abigail wiggled to my hand, holding it next to her face.

"I wanted to be next to Mama," Gabrielle whimpered, tears welling.

Without a word, Abigail climbed onto me and flopped on the

other side so Gabrielle could squeeze in. Ben hesitated, shy almost, and his eyes met mine.

"C'mon." I motioned to the chair. He pulled it next to the bed and placed a hand on my leg.

Like a mama bird gathering them under her wings, I snuggled my chicks near. The intense longing increased as my leveed-up love grappled to pour out. I couldn't express this love. No words, no actions, nothing could come close to the intensity I felt. A love beyond comprehension. I thought, *Maybe all real love flies beyond the ability to adequately share.*

So I did the little I could. I smoothed Abigail's scraggly hair. I kissed Christian's chubby peanut-butter-splotched cheeks. I palmed Gabrielle's shoulders as she rested her head against my middle. I smiled at Ben, beholding him, hoping my love floated through my gaze to his heart.

I also simply took in their presence. As I gazed over them, I realized they were a mess. I chuckled at unmatched socks, dirty shirts, and untied shoelaces. Their breath smelled like not much teeth brushing had happened. Had they taken baths?

I noticed something missing in me. I didn't care. Oh, I didn't care. Normally, these imperfect details would've rushed to my notice—first. I would've scanned the room, checking to see if someone noticed, judged. I might've made an embarrassed comment like "Boys will be boys," or "You can tell their daddy dressed them."

I would've cared about their outward appearance.

Fortunately, none of that happened. In fact, amazingly, and surely by God's grace, something about their very ragamuffin-ness thrilled me. It let their precious spirits shine through. Their imperfectness proffered me the opportunity to delight in *them,* their childlike identity, their jubilant faces, their cherished personalities. I looked on their hearts.

In that moment, I knew my life would change forever. A different mom from the one who entered death had now emerged. New life waltzed through those tough parenting places—the places where I judged myself, where how others saw me as a mom mattered, where checking off my to-do list had risen to top priority, even over loving my babies. With a gentle touch, those areas were swept away.

Truth crystallized. The truth that reading to my Abigail or playing a game with Christian or letting Gabrielle hug me until she was done or listening to music with Ben—those bits, the specks of time, the everyday touches soft as daisy petals—far outweighed the accomplishments fueled by fear of judgment.

I promised myself if I ever felt frustrated as a mom again, I would glide back to this moment when nothing else mattered but loving them.

Chapter Ten

RICKY

And I will give you a new heart, and a new spirit I will
put within you. And I will remove the heart of stone
from your flesh and give you a heart of flesh.
(Ezekiel 36:26)

*A*fter my defibrillator was put in, I had another visitor. My Jesus-loving, faith-healer-enthusiast, gentle-hearted older brother, Rick.

He paced with his typical chill-swagger toward my bed and grinned past his scraggly mustache and shaggy hair. "Hey, sis." He held my hand. Faint cigarette odor wafted toward me, familiar. Welcome exuded from his eyes. I always felt welcomed by him, included, wanted. "You scared us, but God had other plans. Not ready to take you yet."

I squeezed his hand.

He pulled up a chair as I shifted my position. "So they put that thing in you? You don't need it. You have God. I told them not to, but they didn't listen to me."

Weary from the surgery, I didn't answer but chuckled inside. His childlike faith, so fresh, so simple, always conjured a smile. We chatted for a while until Alexandra came in to check my vitals.

When she finished, my brother thanked her. "So what do you do after this?" he asked. "Do you see other patients?"

Her forehead scrunched, questioning. "Yes, I will check everyone's vitals, just as I checked your sister's."

"Would you like me to go with you? Pray for them?"

Kindness flushed Alexandra's face. "Oh, thank you, but you stay here, visit with your sister."

Rick shrugged. "You got it, but let me know if you want some prayer."

Amazing, I thought. *How much he loves Jesus.*

Michael and I sat at a picnic table in a tree-encircled grassy meadow with Rick, his wife, Tonya, and their three girls. A bright Washington sky sparkled in the August sunshine.

I wiped my sticky fingers on a napkin as I chatted with Tonya and the girls. Michael was having a side conversation with Rick, but I overheard. "Do you think marijuana really affects you in a bad way?" My senses perked up at Michael's question. "Everyone says it's good for you."

I thought his question a smidge blunt, maybe even rude, but Rick flicked his longish brown hair back. "Uh, I'm forty-five and working at Subway. I'd say it has a bad effect." He half chuckled.

Thirty years earlier, I was six years old, sitting on the upstairs landing, spying through the wrought-iron railing while my mom and dad argued in the living room below.

"If that kid doesn't cut his hair …" Dad's eyebrows arrowed like a bad guy in a cartoon. His voice rasped. "I won't have a hippie living in my house."

Although not sure what hippies were, I did know they were the opposite of my clean and orderly parents. I may have seen them on TV, maybe sort of like Marsha Brady? But why wouldn't Dad and Mom like the Bradys? I knew Dad disapproved of Ricky. My throat ached, thick and sad.

Then my brother, fifteen at the time, strode up behind me. He always smelled different, sort of sweet, a tinge smoky. Gazing down at Mom and Dad, he shifted toward me. "Hey, sis. Do you want to build a tower?"

I stood, and he took my hand as we headed to my room. His mellow voice comforted me. I reveled in his attention, like a desert longed for rain. I needed him. He loved me without criticism, without bossing, without thinking me an annoying intruder. He liked me.

We heard my parents' harsh voices as they tromped up the stairs, discussing Ricky's having to move out. I peeked at my brother.

"Don't worry, Ocie." He stroked my back. "Dad's in a bad mood."

"Okay."

We settled down on the dappled green shag in my room to construct our tower. Showering me with nice words like what a good tower builder I was, he patiently reminded me of the best ways to create a sturdy foundation and a trippy-looking creation. Finally finished, he held out a yellow triangle. "It's all yours."

I plucked it from his hand and carefully, yet triumphantly, placed it on the top. Gazing at our colorful creation, I wiggled on my knees. "Perfect!" I gushed. "You're the best!" I could never build so good on my own. After a few seconds of admiring it, I giggled. The best part was to come. Without a word, Ricky raised his eyebrows, giving me the go-ahead.

I yanked the bottom block and squealed as the tower crumbled down, spreading out in a ruined pile of primary colors.

That was the last time we built a tower together—the last time

I felt my brother's unconditional love for years. Dad, Ricky's step-dad, kicked him out of the house later that week. Of course, they told me he would be happier living with his aunt. "It's better for everyone," Dad said. I believed him, even though it hurt. But why would my brother be happier away from me?

A few years later, when I was probably in third grade, Ricky finally visited us in our new house. I hadn't seen him in so long that I didn't know how to feel about him coming. Not excited. If anything, a tinge nervous to meet someone I barely knew. I always disappointed everyone, would probably let him down too. I didn't remember how his love had watered my dry heart. I was too young to realize my heart still waited, in scorched dryness, like the desert where I lived.

My mom's silver car pulled into the driveway, and Mom and Ricky walked to the door. His shaggy brown hair still fell almost to his shoulders. After they entered, Mom disappeared into the kitchen, but Ricky paused, smiled at me, knelt, and hugged me. As I toppled into his flannelled embrace, I inhaled a familiar scent—sweet, smoky.

Still kneeling, he touched my arm. "Hey, sis. How ya doin'? You're growing up, girl. Look how pretty you are."

The rush of acceptance saddened and filled me at the same time. His welcome illuminated my empty universe.

I offered a timid smile, then tagged along with him to the guest bedroom. Perching on the brown-and-beige bedspread, I observed him as he unpacked. Opening his suitcase, he discovered a piece of hard candy had stuck to one of his shirts. He grimaced as he plucked it off. "That's kind of gross, isn't it?"

"Yeah."

"Do ya want some candy?" He held out the sticky nugget to me. "It's good!" He winked, and I giggled. He was joking with me, almost like he enjoyed having me around.

During Ricky's visit, I changed, just a bit. At school I had few friends and was often teased, but knowing someone who loved me waited at home … a touch of confidence stirred, began to take root.

In the evenings Ricky would sit on the hearth with his guitar and sing folk songs like "Hang Down Your Head Tom Dooley" and my favorite, "The Cat Came Back."

One night as he sang, a seedling sprouted in my mind. Perhaps Ricky would stay with us—move in. I don't know if I heard the grown-ups talking about this or if it grew from need. It was nothing solid, but a feather of hope floating on the wind, bringing a dream that someone who loved me might settle into my life. Feeling welcomed might be normal.

I carried this hope with me throughout the visit, played with it, watched it grow, and even opened the door to joy.

About ten days went by. Tension ebbed and flowed in our house, so I didn't notice anything different when serious tones filtered from my parents' bedroom in the evenings. Tense foreheads and irritable words didn't warn me.

One night as we ate Dad's barbecued steak and Mom's boiled-up artichokes, we sat silently at the table, watching *The Incredible Hulk* while we dined. A group of hippies snuck into a business and stole a TV, then hung around messing up the place and acting like jerks.

My stomach tightened as disapproval launched from Dad's eyes to Ricky. His scorn finally found words. "You ever gonna cut that hair?" My dad's eyebrows narrowed, zeroing in on my brother. "Or are you going to keep on looking like a creep?"

My brother shook his head mellowly. "Y'know, Dad …" he said, but then he stopped, set his napkin on the table, and walked to his room.

"What's wrong with Ricky?" I asked my mom.

"He's being a jerk." Mom wasn't on Ricky's side either. I didn't think she would be.

After dinner, I found him hanging in his room. He welcomed me, played "The Cat Came Back," and told me he loved me.

The next day when I got home from school, the house was empty, like it was before he came. When Mom came home from work, she told me he'd left. Loss struck me, and even though I fought them, sobs shook my shoulders.

"I'm going to miss him," I blurted out to her.

She frowned. "Don't be so melodramatic."

So I berated myself for showing emotion and recoiled to my room.

After that, I rarely saw Ricky. I heard about him wandering around, a "pothead" as some called him. Eventually he married and joined the military. He served in the army and had kids, but from what little I knew about him, he never found peace, lingered in restlessness.

As adults, we lived only forty minutes apart, but we never bonded again, not like when I was a kid. That day at the picnic, in addition to the marijuana conversation, he also told Michael he could never believe in a God who let bad things happen. His young daughter suffered from diabetes. How was that fair? She didn't do anything to deserve this disastrous disease. No, Ricky wouldn't trust God—certainly not as a father. I wondered if my dad's rejection created obstacles in his course to believe.

So I prayed for Rick. Over the years, my mom had grown to be a strong Christian. She prayed too. Year after year after year, we prayed.

I saw him from time to time, but when first Dad and then Mom died, we lost touch. Nine years passed.

About a year before my cardiac arrest, I spent a busy morning homeschooling, followed by a tense afternoon trying to wrap up an editing job. Dinner finished, I'd just settled into my post-kid time when my phone rang.

"Hello?"

"Hey, sis."

Immediately, I recognized his still-mellow voice.

"Rick! Wow. It's good to hear from you." Then a sick fear hit me. Why would he call after so long? Something bad had happened. "Is everything okay?"

"Yeah, sis, yeah." He paused, took a breath, and my heart raced. "Everything's great."

"Kids are okay? Tonya?"

"Yeah, everyone's good."

"Okay."

"I called to tell you that I accepted Jesus as my Lord and Savior."

I gasped, shocked. "Wha—? What?" Tears brewed, a pang of joy graced my chest.

"Oh, Ocie, I love Jesus so much."

Transcendent hallelujahs exploded into tears that would wait no longer and rivered down my grinning cheeks. A friend from work had shared the gospel with him, a radio show host encouraged him to seek God, and he finally surrendered to Jesus.

My mom's and my prayers—those years we prayed—paraded in my head. "We prayed for you for so long, Rick. Mom and me. For so long."

Now Rick was silent, emotion ridden. "I …" His voice caught. "I didn't know."

"She'd be so happy. I'm so happy for you."

And now, a year later, in the hospital after my death, my brother warmed the spot next to my bed, talking to the nurse about praying for patients, telling me God was stronger than my cardiac arrest, and now …

"Can I pray with you, sis?"

Oh yes, Ricky. You can.

Later that night, after Rick left, Michael came back. He settled into the chair and kissed my cheek. Sitting back, the side of his mouth kinked up, and I knew something occupied his thoughts.

Placing a hand on his warm arm, I sent a questioning look.

The crinkles around his eyes uplifted. "Tomorrow you're going home."

Chapter Eleven

ON THE WAY HOME

And God will wipe away every tear from their eyes.
(Revelation 7:17)

As we drove away from the hospital that Friday in his clunky old BMW, Michael wrapped his hand around mine, his thumb gently rubbing against my skin.

Grogginess still slowed my mind as the weight of what had happened settled. I cherished the idea of going home, looked forward to seeing the kids, my familiar life. But Michael discerned our chaotic, four-kid-occupied house might prove taxing on me. So before vaulting into the fray, he escorted me to a nearby arboretum, gifting me a pause of serenity. As the gravel topped with crispy leaves crunched under my feet, I soaked in the sunshine. The day shone, and that alone amazed me. I lived in Washington State. A sunny day in January? *Just for me*, I thought. My usual self-doubt vanished, not even a glimmer remained on that day.

I arced my hand around Michael's arm as he led my feeble footsteps to a bench, blanketed in speckled sunlight. Still booted up a week before, his broken ankle—because of the surgery—now held him steadily. Only a slight limp remained.

Descending onto the bench, I relished the cool, crisp forest smell. Wintry. Almost smoky. Michael massaged my shoulders, pulling me next to him. He told me he loved me, not so much with words but with his eyes. They exuded adoration like when I'd first woken up.

Always feeling unworthy, I'd cringed at love, the hope of love, even though I longed for its unconditional showers. Over the years, at least in part, I'd learned to receive my Michael's faithful devotion. But I had still doubted, made him prove himself. Yet, now in this place, I swam in his love without fear. My memory of this time is foggy, but I can see petals. Not lush like in spring, but small white friends, peeking their heads through winter's darkness, like hope.

I rested my head on his shoulder, forgetting the forest scents and breathing in my Michael only. His protective arm wrapped around me. He delighted in me—in my very existence. And I reveled in this love, unquestioning, peacefully accepting it. Hoping this new way of receiving love could define my after-death life.

Could I live receiving and giving love so freely? I still had so much to learn.

Along with my two teenage girlfriends, Kathy and Kristy, I strolled over the worn carpet in Elsinore Junior High's library. The sun baked outside, and I soaked in the air conditioning as I palmed the cool surface of the white half-sized book cases. We made our way toward the fiction section where Kristy—perfect skin, brown hair, shorter than me—wanted to show us the Judy Bloom book her sister read, *Forever*. Apparently, it told the story of a teenager having sex for the first time, and we snickered that our school would stock it. The whole idea grossed me out, but I went along—afraid of appearing stupid.

"Here it is!" Kristy pulled the thick paperback from the shelf.

We gazed at the cover, a girl's face enclosed in a locket. We took turns holding it, peeking inside, and that was about it.

"Ew, why do they have that?" Kathy flushed as she awkwardly shoved it back on the shelf.

This whole thing felt wrong, creepy.

"Let's get lunch," Kristy suggested.

With relief, I followed the girls away from that book, toward the door. But before we left the fiction section, I paused. A book caught my eye. The cover showed children passing through two yellow doors into a winter scene. I honestly don't know why I picked it up. Maybe the title enticed me: *The Lion, the Witch, and the Wardrobe*. I'd never heard of it before, but I checked it out.

From page one, I lost myself to this world. The elements in the story ignited my imagination, enchanting my fanciful side. The lamppost, White Witch, Mr. and Mrs. Beaver, always winter and never Christmas, not a tame lion—unbelievable! When Aslan died, I wept. The great lion died? It seemed impossible, but how could anyone escape the deep magic from the beginning of time?

Deeper magic from *before* the beginning of time!

Completely amazing.

Yet, that obvious connection to another world-transforming story didn't occur to me, not yet.

For the next week, I raced through the Narnia books, loving the adventure, the mythological creatures, and especially Aslan. As I finally wound to the end of the final book, *The Last Battle*, evening was falling and powdery light snuck through my gray miniblinds. I lay in my single bed, atop my silky blue-and-white comforter. I turned the last page, closed the hard cardboard cover, and pressed it to me. Tears trickled down my cheeks onto my pillow. How glad I was my parents didn't see me weeping, over a book. Dad couldn't handle it. Mom would be disgusted.

Nevertheless, I ached—for Aslan. "Please be real," I cried out loud. "Aslan, I want you to be real." I longed for him to cherish me like he did Lucy, to call me *dear heart*, and to gently guide me.

Guilt surfaced. Even though my family was not Christian, I'd accepted Jesus a few years earlier, knew I should love him the way I loved Aslan. Then, somehow, with the dark of night closing around me, a light of understanding swept through my heart.

The events of the books swirled to mind. Aslan, the great king; Aslan, the son; Aslan who died and rose again.

Aslan was a picture of Jesus?

Was C. S. Lewis really telling me that Jesus could be like Aslan? Loving and strong, not tame but gentle. Accepting. Close, so close that Susan and Lucy romped through Narnia on his back. Oh, Jesus. Yes, it was Jesus. He loved me like that.

I believed in that moment, but the moment passed. I wasn't in Narnia, but in Canyon Lake, living with a father so different from Aslan.

A bottomless, barren well, its walls cracked from a lifetime of no water—this described my longing. Oddly, some of Aslan's unconditional love stirred the dust in the bottom of this well, made me thirst even more.

When I escaped into that glorious country of Narnia, I sensed the great lion's father-love for the Pevensie children in the way he guided them. He didn't let them wander, venturing to figure out their path for themselves. No, he shepherded them through life's dangers and uncertainties—the concept of a father doing this hovered far, far away.

In sixth grade, when a group of girls ostracized me, I confided in Dad as he drank his after-work martini. Tears drizzled down as I described my loneliness and the brutal words lobbed at me. My hands trembled. In answer, he patted my shoulder and said, his voice tremoring fearfully, "Just don't let it bother you, Ocie. Who cares if they like you?"

I heard, *Stop showing those emotions, Ocie. They scare me.*

If he understood me, instead of offering this trite advice, he would've enfolded me in his arms, listened while I cried and talked, and whispered that he loved the beautiful person I was becoming. I believed that was how Aslan would've guided me. I departed him with my father-love cup empty. For relief, I hid away in my room to munch Oreos.

I longed for an Aslan-like earthly father. I knew I'd never find one in my dad. Given up on that. *Jesus could love me*, I thought, *but how?* How to cling to my heavenly Daddy, to be assured of his love? A lone Christian child in a spiritual vacuum, I didn't know.

As I grew older, that dark, empty well cried out to be filled, demanded to be filled.

Growing to adulthood, as a Christian, I knew I should find that father-love in God, and I did at times. But I could never settle, simply rest, in his love. Like geese in winter always following the same pattern, I swerved back to endeavoring to *earn* his acceptance. My self-righteous self would skulk back, attempting to please using my own contaminated store of "good" works.

So my goal became to hide the grime, the ugly sinful me, the emotionally unstable girl who would lash out at times and then break down in irrational sobs. The one who showed the raw emotion that Dad couldn't handle. The weak, prideful, ridiculous girl whom I hated and who certainly didn't deserve to be loved. This scrambling to mask the real, unclean me in order to be good enough transferred to those who sought to love me. Over the adolescent years, I failed to accept not just God's love but anyone's. This continued till, as a young adult, it even barred me from accepting my new boyfriend's love.

From the moment my heart kindled toward Michael, a fear

lurked nearby, like a villain seeking to blackmail me: *If Michael finds out how pathetic you are, do you really think he'll stay with you? You better be perfect.*

A few months after we began dating, I moved from rural Canyon Lake to big-city Orange County. A friend of Michael's from church rented a room to me. The day after my move, Michael and I hunkered down in the house's living room. Warm sun cornered through the air-conditioned space where my unpacked stuff was strewn over the floor. Michael parked across from me, waiting for instructions.

I needed help, but organizing—not one of my strengths—stressed me. Something he said, I don't remember what, hit a bruised spot in my heart. Worn out, overwhelmed, and scared of this new venture, I possessed zero strength to fight the emotions that thrust against the locks of my "together" façade. The doors launched open, and ugly Ocie burst out in a pulsating mass of insanity.

Tears and snot splotched my face. I spewed irrational words. "You're not helping me." "Why are you doing that?" "Why would you think that would help?" One minute I wept, the next I was angry. He set a box in the wrong spot, and I chucked it like a frenzied toddler. Finally, I crumbled into a walnut-shell ball on the carpet.

Too terrified to peek up at him, I knew what I'd find in his gaze. Disgust. Revulsion. I'd always been rejected when these dark emotions escaped their cell and showed themselves. This would be the end of our relationship. I'd known this day would come. How could I hide my disgusting self forever? He would leave me alone. I deserved to be deserted.

Finally, resolute to get it over with, I rolled to a sitting position, and hugging my knees, I waited.

But I couldn't read his expression. He appeared fearful, yes, but something else. He edged closer to me—not away? Placed a hand on my back. A gentle touch, comforting.

"Ocieanna, it's going to be okay." As he pulled me closer, I nested my head against him. He delicately draped his hand over my hair until my sobs quieted. "I'm here," he whispered. "I love you."

Shame floated away, like a child's let-go balloon. It soared into the big sky as peace took its place. This. The well, so long empty, dried and cracked, this kind of love would fill my well. *This might be what real love feels like*, I thought. *Maybe …*

Never before—not ever—had someone shown me compassion in the midst of an ugly meltdown. Only judgment or needy fear.

Michael lived Jesus' love to me that day, but a desert can't transform into fertile land overnight. It would take years of showers melting the hard clay of my loathsome identity—and even death—before love grew unhindered. Michael's care exampled real, committed love like I'd never known, and as we grew closer, it became clearer that I didn't deserve it.

So, like when Dad favored me, I'd have to strive to earn it.

Chapter Twelve

REST EMBRACED

And behold, there arose a great storm on the sea,
so that the boat was being swamped by the waves;
but he was asleep.
(Matthew 8:24)

Earning love began from my earliest memories and infiltrated my soul through every stage, including parenting.

On a Friday morning at 8:11, a month before my cardiac arrest, I pulled into my son's Christian school parking lot. "You've got four minutes, bud. Run!"

"Why can't you ever get me here on time?" Ben accused.

"You're the one who didn't have your shoes on," I shot back. "Plus, you have four minutes. Better than yesterday."

He hurled an eleven-year-old's eye roll, then hopped out of the van and dashed toward the front door where the principal waited, high-fiving the kids.

Watching him disappear through the entrance, I breathed in, then shuddered as the air released in a presob stream. I hadn't noticed the sadness welling in my chest, seeking exit in tears. I thrust it away.

The adrenaline of the morning rush behind me, I headed to my favorite local coffee shop. I chatted with the cute barista who handed me my cozy warm mocha, then meandered to my favorite spot next to the fireplace.

Within minutes, my relaxed respite morphed into more stress. I drank in a breath for strength, but my anxiety only spiraled further as I stared down my latest editing job—the reason for the aching in my stomach. Well, part of the reason.

Rather than diving into the manuscript, a nicely written Bible study guide that I couldn't appreciate because of the deadline, I pondered how many editing jobs I'd hammered out in a row, one after another after another. The content of these books blurred past me. Deadlines drilled me, compacting my schedule into a rigid prison.

My mind drifted to earlier that morning. I'd forced myself awake at 6:30 and stumbled to my desk next to my bed. Settling into my squeaky wicker chair, I prayed and read the Bible—checked those items off the list. Then, within moments, four-year-old Abigail bopped into my room, full of perkiness, to curl onto my lap. I longed to hold her, to play, tickle … but we had a schedule.

"Time to get dressed, honey," I commanded as I stood, dodging her bid to climb on my lap. "You know I have to take Ben to school."

Her smile melted into a pout. "But, Mama, I want you." Tears pooled in her eyes, depositing more guilt into my gut.

I cupped her soft cheeks in my hands. "I love you. I'm sorry."

She grabbed my hand, not letting me remove it from her cheek.

Finally, I had to break the connection. "I'll see you later, okay? Papa will be home with you today."

She curled up in my bed as I rushed to get ready. The time with her, though cherished, stole minutes I didn't have.

The coffee shop's door jingled as a customer entered. I moaned softly, then placed a hand on my stomach. I'd added mom stress to the work stress, and I'd wasted time. I observed my coffee. Didn't look appetizing anymore.

No solution presented itself to me, no way out of this bondage of stressful busyness. In the midst of our changing economy, Michael had been laid off from his supposedly stable bank job, and although he now worked three jobs, we still came up short each month. We needed the money my editing brought. Normally, I tried to stay positive. At least I worked at something within my skill set, and each paycheck brought a certain pride. I strove to stay appreciative for the ability to help. And I was, really, but I was overwhelmed not just by the work, but by all the responsibilities clamoring for my time and energy, exhausting me, depleting my joy.

Hunkered down at my table, I lifted my eyes over my screen—which I still hadn't worked on—to observe an older man, a regular, lean back in his chair to read the paper. Intermittently, he chatted to the barista or customers as they filed in and out. I decided he must possess an unhurried and relaxed existence.

A throbbing, ironlike lump formed in my throat. To sit and chat over coffee, read the paper, or anything for pleasure. Enjoy my life?

I'd let these thoughts unwind too far. Dreams of a happy life posed a perilous threat to my ability to work—to even finish this particular project. And I had to.

I couldn't allow this emotion in. Ridiculous to complain anyway. Weak. Ungrateful. I stuffed away the unshed tears and forced my attention back to the screen. Again stress cinched my heart. So as I edited, I prayed. Something different this time. Instead of my regular plea for more productivity, I paused my typing for a moment and asked for what my soul longed for—rest. *Please, Lord. I need rest. Lord, please.*

Only weeks later, he answered that prayer.

Welcome Home, Mama! A magnificent kid-drawn banner hung over our garage door. Michael paused the car. His finger stalled before pushing the garage-door opener.

ready?"

nk in a breath, feeling my lungs swell, my heart pump. Tears menaced close to the surface. Today was Friday. Less than a week ago—six days, like creation—I had died and come back to life. God's hand created a new me. A raw creation he'd called out of death's darkness. Out of that sad and lonely night with the paramedics, with Ben crying, with Michael terrified. I could imagine all this. Their fear. Panic. Out of *that* rose a new me. A fresh life.

Staring at the garage door, the dry, barren ache I always carried with me couldn't have been farther away. The water of this new love trickled down, and I wondered how it would spread out, what crevices it would fill. Would it change me? Would it change everything?

There it was again. Hope.

Expectant joy replaced my pensive moment. "Yes, let's go in. I want to see my babies!"

Michael kissed my forehead, then engaged the opener.

We knew that inside the kids would be waiting for the sound of the garage door rising. Sure enough, the door to the house flung open, and four eager faces bobbled, peeking out at Mama. Breathing, living Mama.

As I opened the car door and stepped away from the tomb into my life, I took in each of them. That longing love gushed up, washing over me with heavenly waves of joy. Indescribable. *Oh, Lord, thank you. Thank you for the pulse in my wrist. Thank you for this moment with them … just this moment. Thank you.*

They didn't race into the garage to greet me. Michael probably told them to give me space, but elation beamed from their eyes, their essences. Madcap joy. Their hearts had been empty of their mother's present love for a few days. Fear had sucked love dry. But now … Mama was back! Mama hugs, mama kisses, mama words of affirmation could fill their love buckets once again.

In a whimsical flash, I wondered if their gleeful reaction hinted at how Lazarus' sisters might have felt.

Inside, we plopped down on the couch. The January sun—bright, crisp—warmed our backs, our hair. Abigail climbed onto my lap, pushing her back against me, then shifting to the side, her head pillowed against my heart, her thumb comforting her. Christian clamped onto my left side, played with my arm. Gabrielle latched on to my right, tenderly holding me. And Ben sat next to her.

I reached my arm against the couch to touch his hand. Our eyes met. The same couch where he and Michael watched me disappear into the night in an ambulance. The same couch they knelt before to pray.

I basked in their presence, their love.

"Mama?" Christian pulled back. "What's a *cariack adjust*?" He studied my eyes, so sincere, curious. His cool fingers stroked my cheek.

I patted his cheek like he was touching mine. "Well, my heart stopped—"

"It did?" Abigail blurted. "Your heart?"

Gabrielle sighed. I couldn't see her face, but surely she rolled her eyes. "Didn't you know that?"

"But your heart?" Abigail continued boldly. "That's where Jesus lives."

A mild throb stole across my brain. Energy in my arms and legs waned. As beautiful and soul feeding as this interaction was, it taxed me. I flashed a *help* glance to Michael.

"C'mon, guys. Let's let Mama rest." He shepherded them into the kitchen. "Gabrielle, will you make lunch for us?"

Jon, Michael's brother, and Poppy, his sister, had driven across the country from Illinois to help, because they loved us. They steadied me as I attempted to stand.

I braced onto Jon's solid arm, beneath his Cardinals hoodie, as he supported me up the stairs. He guided me to my room, and I collapsed onto the bed.

"I guess a cardiac arrest really wears a person out." I tried to sound cheery, but this new weak state scared me. Would I always be like this?

Midwestern, thirty-year-old Jon tilted his buzz-cut head. "You okay? I didn't know if you were going to make it up those stairs."

I chuckled. "I could fall asleep after that workout."

"I'll leave you alone, then, but first, let me show you something." He grabbed my laptop from my desk, propped it open, and showed me how he'd downloaded Netflix for me.

"Aw, Jon. You love me, don't you?"

"That's what I'm here for."

With that, he left the room and I fell asleep.

The next day, Poppy introduced me to a cute show. I watched and I slept. Days went by on this TV-and-slumber routine. The household ran well with Poppy and Jon, church friends, and sisters from my homeschool co-op taking care of everything. For a while I reveled in it, feeling content, cocooned in care from others and ultimately from God.

But after a couple weeks, an unhappy thought from my past jarred me. Voices—those nasty haters that lived to tear me down—accused. *You are weak*, they said. *Don't you want to be tough? Don't you want to be the one who overcame a cardiac arrest stronger than ever? That's what people want you to be. A hero, not a lazy bum watching this ridiculous show all day while others take care of your responsibilities.*

I tried to ignore my imagined accusers, to simply rest, cherishing the support my helpers gave, but the voices intensified their attack. *You don't deserve to be content and loved. What have you done to earn such things?*

I crumpled into bed, toggling between enjoying the gracious

care others gave and fighting the voices. Finally, one night after dinner was brought to me, I surrendered. I would prove that I could do more than watch TV and sleep. I planned a series of shining accomplishments. I would get up in the morning, take a shower, go downstairs, and make breakfast. Feats of prowess and action.

The next morning, I got up, took a shower …

And that alone exhausted me. Without even dressing, I slipped on my robe and wilted into a deep sleep on top of my bed covers.

I awoke in early afternoon, rested and filled, renewed by sleep's healing work. A guilty voice nipped at my heart, but I felt too fresh to let it penetrate. I wiped the drool from my chin and noticed a friend had joined me in my slumber. Abigail cuddled next to me.

"Hi, Mama." She yawned and stretched, her hand reaching my cheek.

I kissed her sweat-dampened forehead. "Hi, honey. Did you sneak in here to snuggle with me?"

She giggled and nosed closer. "I like resting with you."

"I like it too. Sometimes it's good to rest."

"You need to sleep a lot, since you've been sick."

Relief drifted over me. Relief that my previous horrid, stressful schedule—the one that imprisoned me a short week before—no longer held me. I allowed myself to remember how miserable I'd existed, sick at heart, tense all the time. In this new life I could rest. Rest.

And I remembered that morning in the coffee shop. That prayer.

I ran my fingers over Abigail's smooth brown hair, welcoming her, not having to push her away. I had prayed—pleaded, begged— for rest.

And I knew. He answered that prayer.

By letting me experience the ultimate "rest."

By bringing me to the stillness of the grave.

By planting me in this room with nothing to do but watch and sleep.

I finally rested.

During that season, I grew to embrace rest. Productivity wasn't as important as loving Jesus, loving my family, loving myself. I could rejoice in these things not because I'd earned the right, but because of something Abigail taught me.

When she snuggled safely next to me, completely secure in my love, when she rested embraced in my arms, she showed me a picture of Christ's care for me. I pondered how many times my Shepherd had called me to rest in his Word. *Amazing*, I thought. *God's rest is not reclining in bed alone, as if left out of the game, as I've been feeling. It's resting in the shadow of your wings, isn't it?* Near him. Embraced by him, as I was embraced by Abigail.

As convinced of this truth as I was, bumps along the path sometimes jarred my way.

Chapter Thirteen

I CAN PRAY

Continue steadfastly in prayer,
being watchful in it with thanksgiving.
(Colossians 4:2)

The cleaning ladies arrived about a week after I got home. I wildly enjoyed these busy bees whom my friend so kindly paid to clean my house. How cheerful the three of them were, how efficient.

I watched one of the flibbertyjibbets on her hands and knees cleaning out my oven, while my fake plants, having been thoroughly rinsed, dried on my pristine island. I'd never thought of rinsing plastic plants. This level of cleaning soared beyond my imagination.

Water ran upstairs as another marvelous cleaning lady scrubbed down the bathroom. The vacuum whirred in the living room, run by cleaner number three.

And me? I watched from where? The couch. I simply remained there, a cuddle blanket on my lap, feeling out of place in my own home. I'd come to terms with resting—feasted on the time to heal and restore. But another week had passed, and a bit of strength returned. I didn't sleep quite as much. I could make my way down the stairs with help once a day.

An aching to be productive pestered me.

Before the cardiac arrest, my whole goal—the thrust of every prayer and plan and thought—revolved around accomplishing things. That pattern, like the ruts in the 5 freeway going south to Portland from Seattle, drew me in as I watched these spunky ladies clean my house. I longed to contribute to the world. Resting was good for me, but what was I doing for anyone else? I couldn't even clean my house.

Before I found a solution, I heard the front door open. A glance at the clock told me it was time for Ben to come home from school. The other three, whom Michael had mercifully taken to a park, were homeschooled, but Ben went to a private school that he loved.

He wandered into the kitchen, where the cleaning lady worked. She said hi, and he awkwardly responded and then swiveled around to find me on the couch.

His blue eyes brightened at the sight of me, and my heart melted. How I relished just seeing my tall-for-his-age boy. His dirty-blond hair. The verging smile hiding behind his lips. I knew he'd be happy to see me. Seeing me would feel like coming home, even more than the sparkly clean house. His heart needed me, and I welcomed that need. I longed to gush love onto him, treasuring every moment with him. That I was here. That I could even look at him from across the room. That he had me to come home to.

He dropped his lumpy black backpack next to the couch, then slid beside me. "Hey, Mom."

I kissed his head. "Hey, bud. Did you have a good day?"

"Yeah." He sighed.

We stayed quiet for a moment.

"Prayed for you today." He rested his head on my shoulder.

"Your teacher is so kind to do that."

"I mean the whole school. In chapel."

"The whole school?"

He nodded and I blinked away a tear.

Gazing at my adored boy, holding him, a memory of something Michael had told me flickered to mind. "Is this where you and Papa prayed that night? On the couch, here?"

He took in a breath and pointed to a spot beside the couch on the beige carpet. "We kneeled right about there."

"God heard you."

"Yeah." He intertwined his fingers with mine. "So many people prayed for you, Mom."

True. I'd been continually humbled—overwhelmed—by the reports of people praying. Our own church prayed constantly. Our denomination sent out e-mail prayer requests. Writing groups, our homeschool group. A friend had a prayer chain going in the Philippines. Someone I knew had family in Japan praying for me. I heard of prayers going up in Australia and England. Years later I still met people I didn't know who had prayed for me during the time of my cardiac arrest.

Awe fell over me, a tightness in my chest. "He loves me," I whispered, mostly to myself. *You love me, Jesus.*

Amazingly, prayers equaled love. I knew that somehow. I felt it. Ben felt it too, God waterfalling his love over us. I patted his hand, and he huddled closer.

✍

Prayer came into my life before I even really knew Jesus. As a four-year-old girl, living in Alaska, I adored my best friend across the street, Natasha. I thought her shiny black hair magical, her smooth olive skin dazzling.

One warm summer day, she taught me how to have a tea party. We perched ladylike in our pink play dresses. Her mom pretended to be our waitress as she served our "tea" (kid-sized teacups of water).

"Sit like ladies," she whispered.

123

I straightened. No one had taught me about sitting like a lady.

"And you hold your pinky out like this." Natasha showed me proper tea-drinking etiquette.

After the pretend tea party, her mother served us canned meat sandwiches. I couldn't tell what kind, but it smelled pretty good. We waited till her mom joined us, and then we held hands and she prayed.

I closed my eyes and bowed quietly, trying to go along with it, act normal, but this whole idea was weird to me. Yet when they spoke their prayer, my heart stirred, sort of like it was thirsty. After the amen, I longed to ask, *Does God hear you?* But fear stopped me.

A couple days later, Natasha and I played hopscotch—another game she taught me—in her side yard. The smell of flowers floated on the slight breeze.

She pitched her rock.

"So, you guys pray?" I said as she hopped.

She kept her eyes on her rock, looking serious. "What?"

My heart raced. I suddenly felt awkward asking. "I mean. Your mom and you … the other day."

Her hair flew as she spun around to head back. "Of course we do." She chuckled like I'd asked a silly question. I felt dumb. Like maybe she was right. It was a silly question. I should know how to pray—but I didn't. I really needed to know.

I picked up my pebble and held it, hesitant to seek clarification, staring at her.

"What?" she finally asked.

Her question fizzled my nerve. "Nothing." I tossed the rock and hopped to the four. But by the time I hopped back to her side, I had decided that no matter how embarrassed, I would make her explain. I had to understand. "How do you pray, anyway?"

A relaxed smile shone from her face. "It's easy. I just talk to God." She circled her gaze back to the hopscotch.

Could prayer be that simple? Excitement like Christmas wiggled in my stomach. "You just talk to him?"

"Yeah."

"He hears you?"

"Yep. It's like talking to a friend, but the best friend ever who loves you more than anything."

This was too much. Could God be a friend? Could he love me? My little-girl mind was blown.

"Sometimes I ask him for stuff. Sometimes I tell him about my day." She seemed so confident, like this prayer thing was a part of her normal life.

A pink leaf from the cherry tree landed on my hand, and we giggled. "Do you want some lemonade? My mom made some."

"Sure."

From that day, I prayed every night before I went to sleep. I told him everything about my day and my life, like a friend. I never mentioned this to my parents or siblings. I didn't know a thing about salvation, redemption, or living the Christian life. I just knew I wanted what Natasha had. Maybe he'd be my friend too.

Please help my sister, Dawn. She's not living here anymore.

Ricky again, God. Help Daddy not to get mad.

Help Daddy come to know you.

Help me be a good girl.

This became a habit throughout my childhood. I liked my friend, and I believed he liked me too.

Throughout the years, in the shifting seasons of my life, I retreated to prayer, but like all of us, I sometimes forgot my friend was right there wanting to listen. I doubted he really heard me, and I lost my childlike zeal to pray.

As I sat on the couch that afternoon with my Ben next to me, the thought breezed to me. There was something I could do. Of course. Yes, I needed to learn to receive, to rest in the love showered on me, but one big conduit of that love was the steady cascade of prayers. If I could splash that love onto others …

I rested my head over Ben's on my shoulder. "I can pray," I whispered.

So, in the same place where my husband's and son's desperate prayers for my life began, I sent up a prayer.

Oh, Lord, I can't do much, but I can pray. Please receive my imperfect words as an offering of love to you. Help me to be content with this calling right now. Even if it's the only thing I can give.

A short while later, I prayed when I lumbered up the stairs. I also talked to my friend Jesus as I closed my eyes to sleep. When I awoke the next morning, joy filled my heart, and I praised my God again for raising me, for the gift of life and breath. Then I waited. *Who should I pray for, Lord?*

As this new "praying me" became a pattern—especially in those early morning hours, slowly waking up—I realized that death was changing the way I prayed in a couple of ways. First, like a song I sang as a child, my sessions with God "bubbled over" with praise. Each morning, with predawn darkness draping me, the happy jolt I'd felt that first morning returned. I awoke almost giddy over how God physically and spiritually rescued me from death. Like the psalmist in Psalm 40.

"He drew me up from the pit of destruction, out of the miry bog … none can compare with you! … 'Great is the Lord!' … You are my help and deliverer."

Also, a new confidence colored my prayers. Like Adam in the before-devastation garden, I gushed my heart out to my Father with abandon, assured of his pleasure in me. Family, friends, acquaintances—even strangers I'd read about—and their needs queued to mind, and like a child placing precious picked flowers into her father's hand, I offered these requests to Jesus: "Here's Ben, Gabrielle, Christian, and Abigail, Father. Michael. Our pastor, our church. And Tami's daughter with skin cancer, and our friends who are single, and the kids in my Bible class, and …"

I imagined him patiently receiving each one, inspecting it, and deciding what would be best. I didn't need to know his answer, just to trust his goodness and wisdom. A new trust—another way my prayers changed.

Those mornings became my delight. How I cherished hiding in the shelter of his wings, loving others through prayers, feeling his grace-dripping nearness. In that closeness, prayers emptied from my soul, freely like water over rocks.

Chapter Fourteen

BIG

Whatever you do, work heartily,
as for the Lord and not for men, knowing that
from the Lord you will receive the
inheritance as your reward.
(Colossians 3:23-24)

Bunched in the blue room with the fifty-two other kids in my Christian high school graduating class, I had to fight back the urge to bounce. After attending public schools through junior high, what a healing balm this school had been. But I was ready to move on! Energy boiled inside. I craved the independence to be a great woman of God to a dying world. God needed me out of this place and in the harvest fields of the world.

The roomful of graduates dizzied with a similar energy, but as they chatted about their graduation parties, an uncomfortable but familiar ache stirred. I wasn't invited to any parties. I shook my head, dispelling these faithless feelings. *A strong Christian doesn't care what others think or do. She focuses on the Lord.*

"Your hair looks awesome." My friend Amy, who had graduated the year before, emerged from the sea of kids. She fluffed my curls, then leaned back. "Gorgeous."

I pulled her into a hug. "Thanks."

"So, make sure when you walk down, you don't trip over your robe. And smile. There's nothing worse than looking all serious in the pictures."

I nodded, wondering if my parents would take any photos. They weren't ones to make a big deal of things like this.

A few minutes later, a teacher herded us into a line, and "Pomp and Circumstance" filled the air. As we filed through the highly decorated gym, through the rows of parents and onto the stage, the emptiness that had nipped at me grew. Something was missing. I was different. My family was awkward, and they didn't love me like the other families adored their graduates. No one cheered when my name was called. *Stop this,* I told myself. *It's a good day. God will use you.*

I spent that summer doing an internship with my Bible study leader. We met at 7 a.m. to pray and study the Bible. We planned Christian concerts and trips to Tijuana, Mexico. We put on Vacation Bible Schools for local churches.

One evening I rode in a fellow intern's Honda Civic. Tami and I were traveling home from teaching VBS to a rough group of teens who soaked up our love and attention yet exuded skepticism about our intense "You must sell out for Jesus" message.

The summer evening dimmed as a pink sunset grazed the sweeping Southern California landscape. I smoothed a strand of hair hanging next to my cheek, then glanced at Tami. Her pretty brown eyes danced. What was she thinking about?

She took in a breath. "I don't know, Ocie. I feel like … I don't know."

I sensed something too. Guessing at what played in her mind, I nodded. "I know. I liked how God used us with those kids. They needed to make Jesus their Lord, not only their Savior."

"Yeah." Her eyebrows slightly narrowed. "I want to do more of that kind of thing."

"Me too."

She tossed her dark hair over her shoulder. "But bigger."

My pulse sailed. "Yes! Big."

We laughed nervously, expectantly.

Thoughts of the Christian music artists, speakers, and spiritual leaders we'd worked with that summer flashed through my mind like a Christian celebrity montage. "If we want to be *big*, we have to really sell out to Jesus, huh?"

She flashed a heavy gaze toward me, then tipped her head in solemn agreement as she refocused on the road ahead.

That was it. The power to be "big" lay in my hands. Be super on fire for Jesus. I could do that!

We giggled as she pulled her car into our leader's driveway, where we would celebrate our VBS week. Excitement built. I knew if I asked God expectantly and really tried, it would happen. "Big" would happen!

Sixteen years later, I sat, my hand over my bulging belly, on the ever-present couch. My kids, ages three and two, rumbled from toy to toy in the bedraggled living room. Since 6:00 a.m., when they'd awoke, my day blurred in a dizzy series of failures—mommy fails, my fails.

Ben, red faced with fists clenched, screamed in my face. "I want more yo-yo!" His word for yogurt.

He'd already had two. I'd said no three times. My strength for the fight waned. I'd just finished washing blue marker from every inch of Gabrielle's body. Her very essence glowed Crayola blue. Ben had cut his hair earlier in the day—a few snips off his bangs, down to the scalp. Then he generously clipped his sister's bangs the same. Lovely. Now two kids would show what a failure I was to the ladies at church—who already knew that anyway.

My emotions spiraling downward, I peered around the room, spying each example of my mommy fails. *Other moms do laundry,* I thought as the seething hot mound of dirties mocked me. *Other moms keep their kids clean. What is that crusty stuff in between Gabrielle's fingers? And how dirty can feet get?* I was going to find out.

Other moms know what they're doing. Not me.

Ben still trantrumed over the yogurt. Gabrielle found another marker, purple this time, and initiated another grand artistry on her feet. And the wall.

Being a mommy was too much. Despair flattened me onto the couch, where I sat staring into space, catatonic, while two tiny people destroyed my life, destroyed me.

Why am I doing this? Questioning thoughts bombarded me. *How did I get to this place of ineptitude? I used to be a strong, competent woman. I thought I'd do big things.*

I laughed scornfully. Those dreams I'd so eagerly sought after had never happened, would never happen. I couldn't even handle my basic mom responsibilities.

Later, after Michael finally came home, I stole away to my bedroom and curled up in the fetal position. I couldn't hold the tears back. I wept uncontrollably over my failure as a mom, as a woman, as a person.

Grabbing my journal with unsteady hands, I decided to stop fighting it. I'd make a list of all the ways I failed. Proof. So I did. As sobs wrenched me, I wrote:

I'm a terrible mom—person. I can't sew. I yell at my kids. I'm not a good friend because I forget to call back. I have no family—mom and dad—to help me, and everyone else does. I forget to give the kids juice. I let them watch too much TV. I'm tired. I'm so tired. I feel alone and I should be grateful for what I have. I complain and cry, when I should be happy. I depend on my husband too much. I feel so alone and sad.

I burn the toast. My kids don't have clean sheets. I forgot to give them a bath for church. My house is unorganized and the dishes are never done. I can't keep up on the laundry. I never will. I don't know where God is. I thought he would help me, but I feel so alone ...

So there it was. I couldn't sew, so obviously I was a horrible mom. I hugged my knees, rocking, as kid squeals—happy or sad, I couldn't tell—invaded from downstairs. And I wished I'd never had kids.

Forgive me, Lord.

❧

I'd been home from the hospital about a month on that pasty white day. Glancing out the window of my upstairs bedroom, I watched as the sun patiently waited behind the sheet of clouds. Hungry for my kids, again hoping to dip my toe in the pond of participation, I carefully made my way down the stairs on my own. Soon the help that had carried my household responsibilities would dwindle. It already had. Could I do this mom-in-charge thing again? Was I ready to run a home and a family? Would I ever be?

I quietly approached the family room. Gabrielle sat at the island, concentrating on a laptop. Christian filled a cup of water at the sink. Abigail perched at the table choosing a crayon to decorate her coloring book.

Glancing around, I noticed a load of clean socks splayed on the couch, washed by the wispy cleaning ladies. Normally, a pile of laundry would form a stew of guilt in my stomach. But now a different blend stirred—joy and opportunity.

As I wended toward the couch, pretty Gabrielle spied me. Her eyes brightened. "Mama? You're down here?"

The others heard and trotted toward me like a troop of happy kittens. I welcomed their hugs as we toppled onto the sofa.

Then as the early February sun angled through the hand-print-bedecked window, like a coming home, or a fresh start ...

I folded socks.

Yes, I did. I dug up two matches—Christian's white ones with stains and a hole in the toe—and folded them into each other. My hands remembered the cotton knit. I smelled the faint detergent. My heart rejoiced that I was here to fold my babies' socks. That I could even do it.

So I held that matched and folded sock bundle before me like a trophy. "Look, guys!"

The kids, who still orbited close by, gazed with awe at my accomplishment. Relief flickered through their faces, saying, *Mama's going to take care of us again.* I was doing what a mom was supposed to do.

We burst out laughing.

"Mama did it!" Gabrielle said in her big-sisterly manner.

Abigail hopped in excitement. "Yay!"

Christian gave me a high five, and we held hands and danced a sock dance for a short moment until I had to sit back down.

I missed the trivial tasks, the mom things, the insignificant chores. In my previous life, these tasks wore on me like necessary, unpleasant wastes of time, but not anymore. Now, far from burdening me, being able to do this one simple chore brought joy, satisfaction, fulfillment.

Then it hit me. Folding socks equaled love.

The tasks I did every day—those tiny boxes on the to-do list—used to be drudgery. I acted as a janitor of our house, cleaning up, checking things off, for no other reason than I had to. Day after day, what was the point?

But now, oh my! Folding socks and all the other chores gained new meaning. I was not a janitor. I was a mom. What I did—all those endless jobs, all of them—meant something. They meant love.

What a joy to embrace this truth. Realizing that each chore I accomplished amounted to an act of love transformed the way I served my family. How much easier it was to get through that stinky pile of laundry, or scummy bathtubs, or never-ending dishes when I knew that doing these things communicated love.

Finishing up the socks, I paused, allowing the kids to enjoy some rare time with me downstairs, but soon weariness fell. I kissed and hugged each one, then asked Gabrielle to shepherd me back up the stairs to rest.

After she left, as I drifted toward sleep, a verse floated to mind. "The greatest among you shall be your servant" (Matthew 23:11).

It occurred to me that this thing I do—being a mom, a house-keeper, a wife—in Jesus' kingdom, is big.

Chapter Fifteen

STRENGTH
OF MY HEART

I woke, the dungeon flamed with light;
My chains fell off, my heart was free,
I rose, went forth, and followed Thee.
—Charles Wesley

Our Sunday school teacher, Mrs. Lawson, stood with about six other third graders and myself huddled on mats at her feet. Sunshine glimmered into the simple classroom through the miniblinds, warming my back as my eyes focused on her. Her short red hair brushed her forehead, and she fidgeted with her papers as she directed us to sit quietly and listen. She acted nervous, like something big was happening, like this moment mattered more than when she told us stories like Noah's Ark, or Father Abraham, or Joseph and His Coat of Many Colors. She was right. This moment changed my life for eternity.

Behind her posed the green flannel board she'd used to walk us through the salvation story. A patch of black symbolized our sin—the things we did wrong. A brown cross explained that Jesus died to take away those sins. Then a robe of white showed that Jesus' death dressed us in nice clean clothes. A flower reminded us of our need to grow by reading our Bibles and coming to church. Then a bright city—heaven.

The simple logic of this story convinced me. I'd been attending Sunday school for about six months, since my friend invited me. She had stopped going, but my mom drove me by myself, dropping me off for Sunday school and then picking me up. We didn't go to the church service.

Sunday school became my favorite time. I soaked in the exciting stories. After Adam and Eve sinned, God clothed them and that serpent was cursed. Abraham almost had to kill his son, but God stopped him. That day when they put the lamb's blood on the doors and the angel of death passed by. What did it all mean? I didn't know, but I embraced each story, so happy to be learning about the God I chatted with in my bed every night.

Mrs. Lawson's latest story—The Story of Salvation, she called it—somehow connected all the other stories. Everything hinged on that one story. I peered up at her from my spot. Her eyes sparkled, but the corners of her lips still twitched a bit. Why was she so nervous?

Once she had our attention, she gazed at us silently for a quick moment, maybe praying, then she said, "If you want to be a Christian, pray this prayer with me." She folded her slightly trembling hands and bowed. "Dear Jesus, please forgive me for my sins and come into my heart."

Of course I prayed that simple prayer with her, out loud. Every ounce of my being had waited for this moment. I wanted Jesus to make me pure like that robe. I wanted the God from those Bible stories to be my friend. *Yes, I'll pray it with you, Mrs. Lawson. Yes, Jesus!*

I don't remember if any other kids prayed, but when we finished, tears moistened Mrs. Lawson's eyes. She smiled at me, then awkwardly (because how does a meek Sunday school teacher act after someone's soul has been eternally rescued?) dismissed us to go find our moms.

In the car on the way home, a relief settled over me. "I asked Jesus into my heart today," I told my mom.

"You did?" She glanced at the sky, then a mysterious peace permeated her gaze. Without looking at me, she said, "That's great, honey. I'm glad."

February came quickly, only two months after my cardiac arrest. Still weary, yet longing to get on with life, I decided to attend my church's women's weekend. White sky granting muted sunlight embraced my hands on the steering wheel as I drove the long, tree-lined road—as straight as the cedars themselves—toward the retreat center. My thoughts unraveled, and a cloud, a tinge gray, passed over my heart.

I'm here, Lord. A hawk, recently home from a winter away, swooped past my car and into the woods. *I'm alive, experiencing your creation.* I placed a hand on my upper left chest, outlined the hard edges of the slightly mounded defibrillator.

The soft shadow settled in, a palpable assertion that I didn't deserve to feel this life. The beauty of the sky, the woods, the birds, the air, my heartbeat, even the way the sun-kissed steering wheel felt in my hand. So many others died of cardiac arrests, but I lived. And not only did I survive, but I also existed in a big circle of blessings. At that moment I couldn't enjoy those blessings. Instead I hauled out my cloak of inferiority, slipping into the groove of worthlessness I'd rolled through much of my life.

My thoughts floated back to a couple of months before my wedding. I had moved to Orange County to the apartment Michael and I were supposed to share after we were married. Late one night,

I had wrestled in my bed, unable to sleep. My chest weighed a million pounds. *I don't deserve to be happy. God doesn't want me to be in a loving marriage. If I really want to serve God, I should suffer for him, especially in marriage. How can I be a woman of God if my life is so easy?*

Ugh. These doubts had wracked me from morning till night. They'd wafted in subtly, a few whispers now and then, but as the wedding grew closer, the nasty beasts got louder.

Until I gave in.

I got out of bed and dialed Michael's number. It took a few rings, but he finally answered, groggy. A part of me cried out, *This is ridiculous! Of course you should marry Michael. He's a good man. He loves you.*

But that proved my point. He was too good. "I think you should come over."

Within fifteen minutes he arrived, worried.

I awkwardly led him to the couch, ignoring his aftershave scent that attracted me. Instead, curling my feet beneath me, I wrapped my arms against my knees. He scooted toward me and reached out an arm, but I stiffened and he pulled back.

No need to prolong this, so I blurted, "I don't think I can marry you." My shoulders relaxed, relieved to finally speak the words I'd felt pressure to say for weeks. Would these words free the chains of guilt? They had to.

Michael's lips tightened, his eyes half closed as he stared away from me.

He didn't ask for an explanation, but I offered one. "You're too good to me. I can't do it." My voice trembled. Sadness, loneliness, fear, guilt rumbled beneath the surface. Where was the relief?

Michael placed a hand on my back, like he did early on when we first dated. My heart clenched. *Breaking it off with him is right. It has to be.*

"I'm going home to my parents' for a while. I want to marry you, but I just don't know if I can. I need to figure out what God wants."

His eyes drooped slightly, but the corners of his mouth tweaked up, comforting. I knew what he was doing. Despite his own hurt, he strove to take care of me. "Okay," he slowly said. "I love you. Take as much time as you need."

So, the next day I packed enough stuff for at least a week. We called the wedding party, warned them there might not be a wedding. I drove away from our life in Orange County, back to the desert town of my youth, sobbing with every mile yet secretly knowing this sadness pleased God.

During my time away, a friend called me. On that foggy morning, I leaned forward in a lounge chair on the deck of my parents' new house overlooking the golf course. I unpacked my situation to her.

"I'm not sure God wants me to marry Michael. I don't really think he does."

"Why?"

I wrapped my arms around myself as the answer quickly flooded to mind. *Michael makes me happy, and strong Christians don't live happy lives. They sacrifice. Put their own happiness last.* But, even as I thought those words, a sharp pang of embarrassed doubt smacked me. Was I doing the right thing? I ventured anyway: "God doesn't want me to be happy."

In a kind voice, she asked, "Why, Ocie? Why wouldn't God want you to be happy? He loves you."

The uncertainty flogging my stomach increased, but my brain didn't quite fathom the question. Why wouldn't God want me to be happy? Well, because he was holy and God and demanding. I had always striven to think of him as a loving God who cared about me, but my worthlessness inevitably emerged. The Christian life wasn't about my happiness—that's what I'd learned, wasn't it? God only cared that I obey, not that I enjoyed my life. Plus, the very fact that I wanted to marry Michael made it automatically against what God wanted—at least that's how I perceived God. It was simple, really.

I fumbled and muttered, but couldn't answer her question. She again spoke truth to me. "God loves you, Ocie. Maybe you should think about that."

A sob pressed, but I managed to thank her and say good-bye.

Sinking back into the lounge chair, I gazed out at the golf course. As rays streamed through the fading fog, I again—as I had for so many years—attempted to dig my grip into my harsh version of God, the one frowning at me, disapproving. But gently, like a father, Jesus pried my fingers loose.

I breathed in shaking gasps, scared to trust him, afraid that if I wasn't good enough, he wouldn't want me. He'd be bothered by me, like everyone else—except Michael. In this state, I finally released my grip, not completely, but enough. The sprinklers clicked on, spraying life-giving wetness over the grassy slopes, and I stepped inside, moved to the wall phone, and called Michael.

"Can I come home?"

He didn't hesitate, and his voice, like the breaking sun warming me through the window, answered, "Come home to me."

I did. And a few weeks later, as I waited to walk down the aisle, the same doubt over my worthiness smacked me again. I walked the aisle anyway, led by my dad, wondering when, if ever, I'd be able to truly rest in love.

This memory lurked as I drove to the retreat. Finding the turn off, I pulled into the gravelly parking lot where I recognized a battalion of minivans. Fellow moms, friends who had been showering their love over me the last month—the first month of my new life.

I wondered if Lazarus had marked off the date of his resurrection. *It's been a month since Jesus called me forth, stinking, decaying. Hard to believe.* Did he feel unworthy of the pulse in his wrists? Maybe he saved the grave clothes as keepsakes, pondered them on his death anniversary.

Entering the hall where I would hear the speaker, I took in the buzz of the ladies, expectantly waiting, happy to have this weekend set aside for refreshing fellowship.

They chatted, moved about so normally as if it weren't a huge miraculous gift to be there, among people—and especially God's people.

I inhaled a breath—weak, frail. Indebted. Humbled.

Soon many women greeted me warmly, and before we took our seats, my dear Kim—the one who was there when I arose—pulled me into a gigantic hug. She'd been driving Ben to school each morning, so I'd been receiving her magnificent hugs each day. How I cherished the love that came through in those squishy, yummy embraces, and I delighted in it just as much now.

She led me to the seat she'd saved for me, toward the back, and I sat down on the cushioned folding chair.

As I listened to the sweet gray-haired pastor's wife, I could barely take it in. The uncomfortable cloud drifted over me again, reminding me I didn't belong in this room with these breathing women.

Why, Lord, did you spare me?

The speaker said something, and my attention twisted in her direction. A verse, "My flesh and my heart may fail, but God is the strength of my heart and my portion forever" (Psalm 73:26).

My soul perked up like a flower seeking ˙
this is about me. The Bible's resurrection sto͟ı
thoughts, each kissing my wounded soul.

Joseph in the pit—down into the deathlike c

the lion's den—sure to die by the lions' hungry jaws. The widow's son—gone, no breath left.

Lazarus.

Christ on the cross.

And yet these stories never end there. Death never wins in God's Word.

Death never wins.

Resurrection came to all of these people. But, actually, even more than resurrection—exaltation. Imagine someone set to die not only resisting the grave, but also receiving more than he had before. Joseph, a hated brother, became second to Pharaoh. Daniel's God was proclaimed throughout the world. Lazarus was physically raised by the Savior of the world. And Christ. Christ sits at the right hand of the Father.

A truth infused me, and then it undid me. Death of God's people always brings exaltation. God breathed life back into my dead heart, but was there more to this journey than just resurrection? Was I destined for exaltation? Somehow this concept crushed the dam barring the billowing waves of his love. Could I accept this heavenly love?

I thought back to that simple prayer with my Sunday school teacher when my first resurrection happened. He loved me then. "You love me now too," I whispered.

And I inched closer to grasping not the so-so, begrudging, obligatory love of my warped, too-small understanding, but a "rejoice over you with singing," an "apple of my eye," an "I will never leave you" love. In nearly inconceivable awe, I glimpsed a speck of God's love that was forged in dusty sandals, sealed in a nail-pierced Savior, proven by an empty garden tomb, and eternalized by a Christ who, ascending to heaven, said, "I will come back for you."

Could this be love like there's no tomorrow?

Chapter Sixteen

A NEW MOMMY

With all humility and gentleness, with patience,
bearing with one another in love.
(Ephesians 4:2)

I giggled like the eight-year-old girl I was as I wiped the wet sponge across the bathroom mirror. *Beautiful*, I thought. *Mommy's going to love my surprise*. She had seemed sad when she left for work, like she was scared about something. I didn't understand anything about her escrow business, but it seemed stressful. I knew her successful job allowed us to live in our nice town with the swimming pool and lake. It helped us go out to eat sometimes. I always had the new clothes I needed. We went to movies. I liked all that, but I wished she could be happier, smile more, laugh. I especially wished she would spend time with me.

She complained about our messy house before she left for work, so after the boiling hot walk home from the bus stop, while Jennifer chatted with a boy on the phone, I snuck to the bathroom. I would clean it just like Mom did, and she wouldn't have to!

Finished sponging the mirror, I moved to the toilet. I sprayed it really good with the stuff Mom used, but then the strong pine scent made my eyes sting. Maybe too much cleaner got on there. I wiped it, but the sponge only smeared the wetness. Mom would get mad if she sat on a soaked seat. I ripped off a few squares of toilet paper. That wasn't enough, so I wrapped a bunch around my hand like a thick glove. That worked. After my last swipe, I gazed at the dry and shiny seat. "Good." Into the toilet went the TP.

I made sure no underwear or dirty socks were on the floor, then skipped to the TV room to watch *Tom and Jerry*. So funny how Jerry always tricked Tom but Tom never gave up.

Mom came home from work, flustered and exhausted, I could tell. She didn't say hi or hug me or anything, just wandered to her room.

Later, Mom and Dad sat on the couch sipping their after-work martinis. I overheard Mom say she had a rough day, but Dad just nodded slightly, stared at her, and then took another drink. Mom's lip pinched, like she was angry, but she didn't say anything, just took another drink.

When they finished, she cooked dinner, and we huddled around our brown table on our wicker chairs, watching *Family Ties* while we ate Mom's spaghetti.

"May I please be excused?" Jennifer, fifteen, flipped her brown Dorothy Hamill wedge cut. "I need to use the restroom." Then without waiting for permission, she left the table.

The bathroom! Excitement bubbled. Jennifer would be amazed at how clean it was, and she'd tell Mommy, and they'd all be so happy with me.

A few minutes later, I heard a watery sound, like something spilling.

"Oh no!" Jennifer yelled.

We all rushed to the bathroom. Dad unclogged the toilet, then he and Jennifer disappeared, back to watch the show, I guessed. So it was me and Mom to clean up. Mom told me to grab some towels from the linen closet. When I came back, she snatched them out of my hand.

"Did you do this?"

My stomach ached. A cry stuck in my throat. "I ... don't think so." I'd so wanted her to be pleased with me.

I made my mommy angry all the time. I wanted her to be happy mommy, but I couldn't make her, even though I tried really hard.

"There was a big wad of toilet paper stuck in the toilet. Did you put it there?" Her voice hardened with the question. So ashamed, I wanted to run away. No, I wanted her to stop, to smile, to tell me it was okay and she loved me. I wanted her to hug me.

I could only stare at her as she continued sopping up the icky water, my voice trapped in my throat.

"You did it." She stopped working and laid her furious gaze on me.

"I cleaned the bathroom." My voice sounded squeaky and ugly.

"Is that why the mirror is all smudged?"

I studied the mirror I had so triumphantly cleaned earlier. It did look smudged, so much that I could hardly see in it. Why didn't I notice that earlier?

Mom would never love me. How could she? My chin quivered. I didn't want Mom to see me cry, but she caught me.

"What's wrong, Ocie?" Again the anger. "Haven't I told you the only person who can make you feel bad is you?" She sucked in a breath, turned away.

"I know," I whispered. It wasn't her fault I felt sad. It was mine.

Leaving the bathroom, I snuck to my room. I muscled back those tears, turned on my TV, and watched it till I fell asleep.

Almost thirty years later, I was the mom. In the early hours of a late-spring morning, before the kids woke up, I had managed to finish an editing job. Such a relief to finish, but before I could e-mail it to the project manager, my two kids, Ben, four, and

Gabrielle, three, burst out of their rooms trailing their usual chaos behind them.

Morning commenced with messy yogurt and Cheerios and a couple of potty accidents. As I tried to manage these and the million other complexities of life with toddlers, my editing project weighed on my mind. It needed to be sent already. But how could I find a second away from these demons? I meant angels.

At the moment, the kids were sitting on the kitchen floor banging on the pans they'd freed from the cupboard. Whatever. At least they were happy. But I couldn't leave them here alone to e-mail that assignment. Staring at their grubby faces, the answer struck me.

"C'mon, kids. It's time for a bath."

Sending that e-mail would only take five (three?) minutes. My office was right across from the bathroom. I'd have eyes on the kids the whole time. Plus, the bath would wash away the dried yogurt and dirt and pee. They loved to splash around in the bath so they'd be happy too. Wins all around! I inhaled victoriously as we marched up the stairs.

Setting the plan in motion—kids in the water, bath toys abundant, warning to be quiet so Mama could think—I crossed the hall to the office, only two leaps away. I watched them as I clicked open my e-mail. They giggled and played. My shoulders relaxed.

I found the address and file. Attached.

The kid volume rose. Still sounded pretty happy, just loud. Growing louder.

I clicked Send.

Kid volume climbed to very loud.

The blue line indicating the e-mail was sending moved super slowly. My e-mail wasn't going through.

"Kids, you need to quiet down!" I yelled, as controlled as I could manage. But my pulse raced and stress restiffened my shoulders.

Error message. Something was wrong with my e-mail. I had

to figure it out, but now high-pitched screeching hailed from the bathroom. "Just give me a minute!" I screamed back, saying adios to the control I had labored for.

The e-mail wouldn't go through.

My ears started to bleed from the wailing going on in the bathroom. I could see them. They sat there—safe—but howling like their arms had been ripped off.

This e-mail. I had to send it. It would only take a few minutes to fix. But with all this lamenting coming from the bathroom, I couldn't think! Anxiety rose to red level. Self-control vanished, and I marched into the bathroom.

"What is going on?!"

"The soap is in our eyes!"

"Soap?" I used kid-friendly, no-tears soap. Why would that make them wail like the end of the world? I looked and saw a bar of grown-up soap floating in the murky water.

My rage climaxed, but I found restraint again. "Oh, kids. That must really hurt. Mommy's sorry. Let me help you."

Ha! Not really. I wish that was what I said, but instead a white-hot yell seeding in my stomach boiled up to my mouth and erupted. "You stupid kids! Haven't I told you to never touch grown-up soap?"

This calmed them right down. Not. Their eyes rounded in shock, scared by this mom betrayal. They cried and cried, broken-hearted tears dripping into the soapy water.

"I want a new mommy," Ben sobbed.

And, finally, by God's grace, my heart softened. Guilt sludged over me. I left my e-mail floating in cyber limbo and focused on these two poor babies. "I'm sorry, guys. Mommy should never talk to you that way."

"We forgive you."

They cried as I held their slick, wet bodies.

I dried them, tended to their stinging eyes, and prayed. *Oh, Lord, this is not the mommy I want to be. I never want to yell at them again. Please help me.*

God didn't magically fill me with the self-control to never yell again, like fuel filling a gas tank. Stress worn, I still snapped when tugged and yanked too far. Overcoming this anger became a humbling journey of crying out to God. Many fun, touching, happy moments were interspersed with frustrated outbursts. Some improvement occurred as I sought Christ's help, but I longed to love them better, to pour grace and joy on my kids.

After I died, my heart so overflowed with love that I didn't grump at all. I'd see my kids and be filled with joy. I wanted them around me. Climb on me, sit next to me, tell me your stories, ask for my help. I want you!

About four weeks afterward, I was getting back to "normal" life, taking care of things, being a mom. The help from church and friends had slowed way down.

Still easily weary, I did what I could, and I needed the kids' help. One morning, the clouds gloomed charcoal gray outside as I scrambled eggs, set the table, and fed them by myself. Michael had left before sunrise to go to his first job. Ben was at school.

Weariness scratched at me, and my thoughts became focused on getting back upstairs to rest. In my mind I was already there, not where I should've been—present with the kids. We finished eating our egg burritos and the kids popped up to play.

I gazed at my two littlest ones, ages six and four. "Okay, Christian and Abigail, I need you to clear the table." Then I shifted to Gabrielle who was ten. "I'd like you to do the dishes. I need to rest."

They all nodded. "Yes, Mama."

"When you're done, get started on your math, okay?"

I left to join my mind up in my room. Ah, the bed. My eyes closed, my body relaxed. Rest.

About an hour later I flitted back downstairs, expecting to see the kids studiously adding and subtracting around a spiffy kitchen table. But it wasn't spiffy at all. Not a speck of spiff. And they weren't doing their math, but watching TV.

They ran to me, happy, when they saw me, wanting hugs.

I didn't welcome them, but glared. "You guys didn't do what I said!" I snapped. "I can't believe you disobeyed me, even when I'm sick. Thanks a lot." Passive aggressive—my modus operandi.

Oh, how sad their faces looked. Disappointed and even—the worst—surprised. Their eyes said, *I thought you weren't going to do that anymore.*

Immediately my heart softened. I could almost hear the Holy Spirit say, *Love them, Ocieanna, like I do.* The verse—that eternal verse that embodies who God is, that pulleys through the Bible like a grab rope—came: "The LORD, the LORD, a God merciful and gracious, slow to anger, and abounding in steadfast love" (Exodus 34:6).

Slow to anger. *Abounding* in steadfast love.

Tears burned behind my tired eyes. Tears of sorrow for my sin, and humble rejoicing in a God who was slow to anger. He was all that I was not. His patience with my repeated sins literally brought me to my knees. I crouched before my wee ones, apologized, hugged them, and carried/dragged them to the couch. I spent the next few minutes tickling and telling them how wonderful they were. More hugging, kisses, laughing, and love.

Abounding in steadfast love. Oh, how loving them diffused my anger. God shared the answer to my anger. Love instead. Abound in love. Overflow, don't withhold it. Pour it down like rivers in springtime.

As we basked in each other's presence, I knew, deep in my soul, that I didn't have time to be angry. This moment, every moment, would die away, like even the most glorious daffodil shines for a mere twinkle. How could I spend this rare treasure mad, when my God exuded not anger but love? How could I squander the time God had so graciously gifted me. I hugged my arms. Sobs gathered. *I will worship you forever.*

Then another ray ruptured through. Someone else could be making my kids breakfast. Someone else could be training them to follow directions, to clean, to be respectful and compassionate. My mind swirled through the chain of mom stuff. Someone else could drive them around, teach them, take them to co-op, help them with schoolwork, untangle knotted hair, and so on.

Again, that original longing love flooded my heart.

I stilled, leaning back, and drew a breath. "I'm here, guys." Abigail shuffled onto my lap sideways, tucked her thumb in her mouth, and leaned her head against me. Gabrielle and Christian nestled on either side. My fingers trailed over their shoulders, arms.

The memory of my mom's anger disquieted the moment. How small, helpless, worthless I felt under the force of her rage. *Lord, I don't want my children to feel like that.* I kissed Abigail's head. *I don't want to be the reason they feel like that.*

Help me to love them like there's no tomorrow. Help me to love them like you do.

Chapter Seventeen

HUMILIATION

Consider the lilies, how they grow:
they neither toil nor spin, yet I tell you,
even Solomon in all his glory was not arrayed
like one of these.
(Luke 12:27)

Relaxing in the back seat of my friend's SUV, warm air whipped my hair but I didn't mind. The breeze minimized the early July heat as three friends and I trekked home from a four-day homeschool conference. With the wind hindering our conversation, I fought to capture anxious thoughts. The conference refreshed me with renewed resolve to teach my kids. I also drank in the fun with other moms on the loose, but an underlying dread followed me as well.

Six years before this trip, after years of struggling to find a job that fit Michael's skills and our budget, the Lord had blessed us with the perfect position at a well-established, solid mortgage company. It was his dream job. During his work as an independent broker, he'd heard of this bank and loved their low-interest, stable loans. No subprime with this group. Michael was proud of that.

How I relished the steadiness of a constant income flow. For several years before, we'd survived on commission only, never knowing how much we'd have to live on the next month. But now, taking care of our home, providing necessities for the kids, sharing with others, and having modest but regular recreation time became our normal pattern. We even packed up our green van and jaunted down to Disneyland one fall to create memories with our kids.

Money didn't overflow, but we had enough. A sense of security, absent for years, finally settled in, and my footing seemed sure. Not stressing about money freed me to creatively care for my home and kids. How I cherished this! Jesus was blessing us. At first, I worried that, since I wanted this financial security, he would rip it from me, but slowly I trusted his care. He provided, and I could be a normal wife and mom living a normal life in suburban America.

But then the financial crash of 2008 happened. Banks closed. The economy careened into the muck, and even the sixty-year-old award-winning establishment Michael worked for faltered. Rumors of layoffs circled, but since Michael had been promoted to branch manager, we hoped he'd skirt the layoffs. When the company sold out to another bank in the summer of 2008, rumors rumbled even more. Fear of the inevitable bombarded me as my friend pulled in front of my house to drop me off.

Trudging in the door through the late-afternoon heat, I spied Michael descending the stairs to greet me. I knew by the look on his unshaven face that the waiting was over. The worst had happened. He held me, and we sought the Lord. He would take care of us. Michael had strong skills. He'd been promoted in every company he worked for, managing several times. I was scared but also determined to trust Christ and Michael.

Three years later, I sat in Michael's car in the parking lot of the food bank. My mind swam, drenched in despair, as the welled-up sobs finally escaped into gasping wails. Examples of our need pummeled me with repeated blows. Not only did the van need repair, but the kids' clothes were also threadbare and too small. They needed haircuts. Last month we mustered up enough money to repair the broken fence, but the cracked window waited to be replaced, unsafe. My bedsheets had holes in them. The ceiling fan in the dining room died and messed up the wiring—half of the downstairs had no electricity. Our fridge leaked.

Stop, I told myself. *No point going over each failure. You'll never finish such a list.* I commanded myself to refocus on Jesus and his care. But in moments of insecure panic—moments like this—the old lie slinked back, telling me that my sin and weakness caused God to shut the gates of blessing. These thoughts scratched at my gates as I wept in the car.

But even more than guilt, on that morning anger reigned.

Anger that we'd tried so hard for three years, but God declined to bless the work of our hands.

Anger at myself for giving in to despair and frustration with God for not granting strength to rejoice in suffering.

Anger that our van's transmission was broken and we had no way to fix it.

And in that moment, I raged, boiled, fumed over the fact that the only way for me to provide Christmas presents for my kids was to come here, to the food bank's Christmas gift program, where I would embarrassingly receive the charity of others.

Still resentful but resigned to get it over with, I wiped my damp cheeks, checked the mirror for smudged mascara, and stepped out of the car. I arrived to the storefront they'd rented for charity Christmas present distribution four minutes late for my appointment, so I had to wait for them to squeeze me in.

Without a look around, I withered in shame. I thought of Mom and Dad, who had both passed away years before, and the comfortable life they'd worked for. I could see my mom's disapproving frown in my mind's eye. I sighed. *At least they never saw me so pathetic.* A bitter squall threatened to burst through again, so I forced a cloak of numbness over myself until a lovely lady, a mom like me, dressed in cute clothes and sporting an awesome fake blond hairdo, appeared.

"Hi, I'm Nancy. I'll be escorting you through the gift tables." She shimmered with sweetness. "Like a personal shopper."

Humiliating. I was her age. Raised with nice things and good hair and stylish outfits. But now I slouched in charity clothes. I couldn't afford a haircut, much less color, so my grey-streaked locks flopped in overgrown shapelessness. Nancy embodied who I should have been. Used to be.

Numbly I tromped through the big room, picking out gifts, then thanked Nancy and drove home, feeling a bitter gratitude. *Will this never end, Lord?*

After my death experience, people asked me how we would pay the medical bills so often that I began to worry. I doubted treatment for a cardiac arrest could be cheap. One morning, as Michael parked on the bed pulling on his work shoes, worry built to anxiety. I shifted from my spot at my desk.

"Hey, babe," I cautiously probed. "How much were the medical bills?" I held my breath, not sure I wanted to know the answer.

"One hundred and twenty thousand dollars," he said, brushing his pants as he stood. "Why?"

Panic wracked my body, but I fought it down. "How much do we have to pay?"

"One hundred and nineteen thousand dollars," he nonchalantly answered.

"What? Why?" Every emotion flailed me—shock, anger, despair, fear. "That can't be right!"

He eyed me, confused. "I think it's pretty good."

"Wha—?" I was lost. "Why aren't they paying more?"

He paused and approached me. "Did you ask how much we have to pay or how much Medi-Share is sharing?"

"How much we have to pay."

He laughed. I wasn't laughing. "We only have to pay one thousand. The Medi-Share members share everything else."

Sobs burst out of me—ardent, loud, gnashing sobs. Tears dripped through my fingers as I held my hands to my face, completely overwhelmed. Again God showed me love through death. His love was so intense. He hadn't abandoned us. He hadn't forgotten about our poverty. He was keeping his promise to take care of us. Why had I doubted him? He never failed.

Poor Michael pulled me from my desk to sit next to him. I nuzzled my head against his chest and wet his dress shirt with my tears. "God's taking care of us," I blubbered.

Michael patted my back. "He sure is, darlin.'"

That day I wrote a thank-you note to Medi-Share.

Yet, still on the edge of financial ruin, I struggled to trust, despite the moments when evidence of his care shone through.

At one point during our time of meagerness, I ate lunch with a group of women I considered friends. Financial stress' rough claws still held me. The fight to cling to Christ had worn me down, and at least for a time, I succumbed to despair. As I spoke with these women, I decided to throw open my cloak of invisibility and reveal my wounds. Maybe Christian friends' support would deliver some of the comfort I craved. Maybe they could help me back to my trusting place.

"So, our van broke down. Four thousand dollars." I decided to open with the big one.

Emily, another mom whose husband worked at a large Seattle software company let out a slight gasp. "Oh man, that's a lot. I hate it when something like that happens. Who has four thousand dollars lying around?"

I tried not to think about the amazing trip she and her family had recently returned home from, not that I resented her. I was happy for her—truly—but a big vacation like that soared far beyond my reality. I didn't think she or the other women grasped the disaster that the van's demise represented.

I tried to explain. "We're not making our bills as it is. We have to use credit to pay the power company." My heart pounded, and my hands quaked under the table. I felt so incredibly vulnerable. Naked. Ashamed.

Another mom, a young blonde with a cheery demeanor, leaned forward. "I know. Things are rough for us too. I had to cut my grocery budget, and we can only go out to eat once a month now—you know, to the expensive restaurants. We still go to fast food when the occasion requires."

All the ladies chortled.

"Sometimes you don't have time to cook," someone agreed.

They weren't getting it. How could I explain that these weren't the normal financial hurdles of raising a family? Complete financial crisis loomed like a ready-to-erupt volcano. I blurted out, "I don't have a garbage disposal!" Surely this would show how poor we were. We couldn't even afford to replace this minor appliance. I didn't mention all the other broken appliances and basics we lacked.

Confused stares, then another gal who was my age frowned. "Do you really need a garbage disposal? I often think how lazy we are in America."

Lazy? I was lazy? Honestly, I didn't care about the garbage disposal or all the other things we lived without. The tender pain throbbed not from the deprivations themselves, but from what those deprivations symbolized—my complete failure. I had failed to provide. My husband's hard work was not being honored. God, whom I trusted to care for me, had forgotten us.

I staggered to the bathroom and cried.

I knew she and the other ladies didn't mean to hurt me. The type of suffering I endured resided far outside their reality.

Fortunately, not everyone reacted this way. During this time, one friend provided an oasis of lived-out love. When Mary heard about our family's money burdens, she gently approached me and simply asked for a grocery list. I hesitantly gave her one. The next week she brought us coolers of food—good food that made me feel normal again, more than I'd asked for. And paper towels and even Kleenex—the soft, easy-on-the-nose kind. She spoiled us. Even the cheap, rough kind of tissue never made it into my paltry cart. Too much of a luxury.

Mary's love brought a respite from the shame, but I still grappled to trust. Yes, God was providing my daily needs, but like the Israelites who grew tired of manna, I so longed for more than only the next day's provision. I ached for a sense of stability. *Oh Lord*, I constantly cried, *please give us a normal paycheck. It doesn't have to be a lot, but something regular I can depend on.* Yet weeks went by, months, years.

And his answer was no.

To be honest, although God continues to provide in many ways, even now, years since the cardiac arrest, I still battle to rest in God's provision. Our finances didn't get better after my "event"; they worsened. Of course they did. I stopped editing, so no income flowed from me, and then the company Michael worked for shut down and he again lost his job. As our finances continued to plunge, my pattern of trusting for a time and then falling into shame and despair continued.

But not too long ago, a truth, like a breeze tickling summer leaves, drifted into my soul, gifting me a handhold to grip. Something like hope.

A couple of years after my cardiac arrest, we switched to a new church. As much as we appreciated our former church home, we rejoiced in our new congregation as well—still conservative Presbyterian, but a cozier church plant. Hope first wafted in during a worship service at our new church. As our young pastor carefully guided us through Genesis, he uncovered a theme true from Adam and Eve to Sarah and Abraham to Jacob and Rachel all the way to Joseph. Each of these patriarchal units launched their journey in a place of blessing, honor, and privilege. They all lost that position.

As we plodded through their lives, we experienced this pattern. Pastor Dan shone at compassionately reminding us (or me—it seemed like he spoke just to me) that Jesus never promised to forge away the spiky ground, but to shepherd us through, maturing us as we, battered and bruised, trekked the treacherous fields. As he guided Abraham, Jacob, and the others, he would lead us (me).

One particular Sunday, as I sat in one of our church's red velvet chairs, worry of finances physically pressed. My heart ached. My throat stung with unreleased sobs. As the sermon, surrounding an example of Jacob's many hardships, wound toward the conclusion, Pastor Dan reminded us that Jesus suffered too.

I knew about Jesus' suffering, but as Pastor Dan circled closer to his main point, my pulse sped up and my chest throbbed in anticipation. Hearing about my Savior's compassion when my heart ached so intensely—this might be dangerous.

He continued. Even though Jacob's scheme to manipulate his brother from the birthright gained him a legal standing in the family, he lost everything else. Had to flee not only from his home and his brother who strove to kill him, but also from the land of promise—the land where God met his grandfather Abraham and his father, Isaac. The land of God's presence. Instead of dwelling in blessing, he wandered, eastward, through the wilderness, to a place where he had to work not as a son but as a servant.

Here comes the part about Christ, I thought.

Jesus the King of heaven also descended from a place of high status to walk this dusty earth in humility. But unlike Jacob, Jesus did so willingly—for us.

Pastor Dan continued, but I camped out there. Something about the concept of Christ lowering himself to love us where we live shattered me. Tears splashed from my cheeks to my hands.

As Michael drove us home from church, I gazed out the window of our minivan at the winter sun streaking through gray clouds onto Lake Washington's whitecaps. *Why did that hit me so hard, Lord? I've heard it a million times.*

Ever so slowly, meticulously, the light of understanding angled through.

I grew up in a comfortable home. I knew an easy life in regards to material things. My parents had enough money to fix broken appliances without a thought. If I needed clothes, my dad handed me a wad and let me shop. We could buy any food we wanted. My sheets never wore so thin that holes formed in them. We always had a garbage disposal.

I'd fallen from that. I knew others suffered much more than I, but for me, losing many of the normal comforts of modern American life left me ashamed, insecure, not sure of my identity.

More than anything else, this fall embodied *humiliation*. As we floundered through life as poor people pretending to be like our middle-class friends, that word hung on me like a dirty T-shirt. Everything humiliated me—to ask for help with our homeschool co-op fees, to have to volunteer in order to afford a writers conference, to receive money from the deacons' fund, to watch the offering plate pass by week after week because we didn't have one penny to put in, and on and on.

We continued our drive home, and I studied the trees lining the lake. Most were naked from the winter winds. A passage came to mind.

> *Have this mind among yourselves, which is yours in Christ Jesus, who, though he was in the form of God, did not count equality with God a thing to be grasped, but emptied himself, by taking the form of a servant, being born in the likeness of men. And being found in human form, he humbled himself by becoming obedient to the point of death, even death on a cross.* (Philippians 2:5–8)

These words breezed through my thoughts, my heart. He emptied himself. Taking the form of a servant. Humbled himself. On a cross.

So ... I breathed in shakily.

Maybe my fall from middle class was ...

Could it be?

An honor.

My plunge into suburban "poverty," instead of proving God's disapproval, disinterest, or absence, gave me the privilege of sharing in his sufferings? In a small way, yes—tiny compared to his sacrifice. But even my scant suffering (which didn't seem so small to me) allowed me to participate in Christ, to identify with him, to serve him.

So like with all those Genesis saints, the miserable fire during those years of want refined me. He used those tearful, tormenting times for my growth, to humble me, to draw me into his arms and remind me that I don't want for anything, really, because the King himself—the one who surrendered his heavenly home to endure the suffering I deserved—well, he's my Shepherd, and even though I may have nothing in this world, I am blessed with everything I need in him.

I relaxed my head against the seat, letting this truth soak in, but then a touch of fear reemerged like choppy waves' relentless rhythm. *I don't know if I can live in this trusting-in-suffering place, Lord. Not always. I'd rather this suffering end. Will it ever?*

No clear answer came to that question, but I already had an answer, just not the one I wanted.

Help me to again trust that you love me, Lord.

Chapter Eighteen

THE LAST CASSEROLE

But now thus says the LORD, he who created you,
O Jacob, he who formed you, O Israel: "Fear not,
for I have redeemed you; I have called you by name, you are mine."
(Isaiah 43:1)

One evening about a month after I returned home, the kids scampered off to play and I leaned against the cluttered island, my hand landing on something sticky. I ignored the goo and the rest of the mess, instead eyeballing the oven.

I'd put in a glorious casserole a dear sister in the Lord had made. A beautiful creation with cheese and peas and noodles and chicken, it mounded large enough to feed all six of us and still provide leftovers.

But it was the last one.

For a month—a month!—I hadn't worried about making dinner. Such a relief and blessing. Receiving such scrumptious meals almost made having a cardiac arrest worth it.

Now that the last casserole commenced its transformation in the darkness of a hot oven, what would I do? I slouched down on the stool next to the island.

I'm going to have to fix dinner again. As my mind clipped

through the steps to cook a meal—planning, shopping, chopping, assembling, stirring, checking, serving—oh, my stomach ached. I was still recovering, still weak. Could I do this?

This fear didn't stay isolated long. I gazed around the destroyed house. *Can I do any of this? Can I manage a home again? Be a wife, a mom, a friend, a homeschooler, a teacher, a writer?*

I touched the sticky spot on the island counter. Without thinking, I stood and grabbed a sponge. Doubt infiltrated my being.

Who am I postdeath? Will I ever be me again?

Anyone who grew up in Southern California in the seventies and eighties couldn't have missed this ever-present jingle that played incessantly over television and radio waves:

If you're looking for a better set of wheels,
I will stand upon my head to beat all deals.
I will stand upon my head until my ears are turning red.
Go see Cal. Go see Cal. Go see Cal.

Cal Worthington and his "dog" Spot (some animal, like an elephant, tiger, pig—he frequently changed it as a joke) would frolic in front of his car dealership singing the catchy tune. He wore a broad white cowboy hat and a big car-salesman's grin. Sometimes he actually stood on his head. Cheesy, but effective. Everyone knew that song.

Including the kids at Elsinore Elementary School.

Having completed a typical day in third grade, I strode toward the bus line. The aging school had no air conditioning, and temps would soar past one hundred degrees. Sweaty and exhausted, I approached the long yellow bus. A wad grew in my stomach, like sticky gum making me ill. The last place I wanted to plant my bum was in a cramped vehicle full of other perspiring bus monkeys.

Before I could step on, a group of girls pushed ahead of me, knocking me back against the chain-link fence and making me drop my books. Numb, I simply picked them up and took my place in line.

After plodding up those big steps, I gazed over the sea of kids. *Ugh, it's almost full.* My normal spot, third row on the right, was filled, so I cautiously strode toward the dreaded zone—The Back. Sixth graders remained in The Back, standing up while the bus moved, yelling out coarse jokes, and doing other scary things I didn't understand—didn't want to understand.

Everyone looked the other way as I inched along, not wanting to make room for me. With every step, anxiety rose. Finally, I spotted an empty seat in the second-to-last row. A girl sat there, a fifth grader. To my relief, she smiled faintly and moved her stuff for me to sit down. Without speaking to me, she refocused on reading a book. I sat down, my bare legs sticking to the green vinyl. With fingers gripping the cool metal bar under the seat, I concentrated on my only hope. *In thirty minutes, I'll get off, walk home, eat Oreos, and watch TV.* I just had to get through the next thirty minutes.

The bus driver closed the door, and the wheels on the bus turned as it edged away from the curb and started down the street. Once we got on the freeway, the Back Seaters started in.

An oversized, shaggy-haired kid whom I recognized as the main troublemaker stood up and whacked a short boy in the head.

"Hey!"

I knew the short kid. Alex, the class clown—or bus clown. He joked and acted weird and made people laugh. In retaliation, Alex let loose a torrent of balled paper at the tall kid, hitting him in the face. Everyone cracked up. Including me.

That's when Alex noticed me. I shouldn't have laughed, instead keeping my head down and staying below the radar, but it was too late. He marked me curiously, his mind working. "What's your name?"

Oh, my stomach ached. I didn't want this attention. "Ocie."

Without a moment's thought, Alex sang the Cal Worthington song. "If you're looking for a better set of wheels …"

I stared at him, confused. His face held a devilish grin as he sang. Then, after he mimicked the beginning, he smirked at me and shouted out, "Ocie Cow. Ocie Cow. Ocie Cow."

Snickering cackles erupted. Gazes drilled in on me, mocking, exulting like kids do over silly jokes. Soon others joined in. Everyone sang, over and over, "Ocie Cow. Ocie Cow. Ocie Cow."

To me, all kindness had been sucked from the world. Why would they call me a cow? I wasn't one of the chubby kids, who were so relentlessly teased. Was I ugly? Stupid? Nerdy? As I kept still, trying to act like I didn't care, I wondered if any kid's heart bent with compassion for me.

I glanced at the girl sitting next to me, the one who had let me sit down. She too tittered and sang along, then caught my eye and mouthed *sorry*. I understood. She feared being the next one singled out. Maybe she realized the social catastrophe that had just happened—as I did.

After what seemed like hours, they stopped singing and moved on to something else. Yet my humiliation hung on. Eventually the bus came to my stop. As I made my way down the aisle to the gateway from this torture, kids along the aisle said, "Bye, Ocie Cow," and "See you tomorrow, Ocie Cow."

Plodding home under the ovenlike desert sun, confusion snaked through my mind. Until then, I'd still accepted my dad's adoration of me. If he was right, and I shone with awesome specialness and unrivaled beauty, why would my peers degrade my name, mock me like that?

I played the bus scene over in my head, and the "truth" became clear.

Dad was wrong.

His doting words came from his skewed love for me. They weren't reality. I wasn't beautiful, smart, special …

That day, the old me, the one who still endeavored to cling to Dad's shining opinion, gave up. And gave in to the lie that would whisper around me for years. I was nothing but a worthless cow.

So, Ocie Cow became my name. No one said, "Hi, Ocie." No one said hi at all. They didn't want to associate with Ocie Cow.

Years later, in junior high, I was still known as Ocie Cow. During that time, I delved into the Bible for myself and noticed a pattern. God changed people's names—Abram, Jacob, Simon, and others. Why did he do that? I didn't know, but this name-changing trend intrigued me. Also, he bestowed this new-name gift while they still behaved in distrustful, weak, even rebellious ways. How did they deserve such a blessing?

I craved a new name. "Ocie" was associated with Ocie Cow, and I hated its ugliness. I didn't like Ocie, the weak, unlikable person either. Would God rename me? Change me into someone worthy of this gift?

After high school, I wanted to be a missionary—one more strategy in my scheme to please God—so I enrolled in a ministry course at California Baptist College. As freshman year wound toward summer, a question played in my mind. *To be a missionary, do I even need college?* Friends had flown off on far-reaching mission trips. I'd already journeyed to Scotland my freshman year of high school as a teen missionary, so why not just go? Not long after this seed presented itself, it bloomed.

At home one weekend in early spring, I announced to my parents that I would quit college and take their money to go to the mission field. I wish Mom and Dad would've told me if I expected them to pay, I had to finish college first. But saying no to me wasn't easy, especially since I explained how God had directed me to switch paths. How could they argue with God? So instead of entering my sophomore year, I boarded a plane headed for Hawaii to be used (and loved—I hoped) by God.

The first three months of this six-month trip consisted of morning and evening lectures in Maui. When this time ended, our team set out for "outreach" in which we traveled from Hawaii to a group of small Pacific islands called Micronesia. Our first stop was Saipan.

I adored this experience. The sun-drenched island lingered in tropical glory. The people exuded both outer and inner beauty, and I fell in love with their bright eyes and hospitality. Plus, I delighted in the times we reached out to the community, mostly by doing skits and acting out Christian songs. I was finally really serving God. *You're happy with me now,* I prayed as we bounced home on the rainbow-painted bus after an evening of ministry. *I'm doing this for you.*

But later, as I lay in the girls' barracks on my stiff bottom bunk, the chilling truth wouldn't be silent. To the remote reaches of my soul, I knew even this missionary work failed to please a holy God. How could my works—even my most radically Christian efforts— ever please him? As the tropical birds' songs seeped into our room, I emptied my fears to God. *I'm trying so hard, Jesus. Please don't abandon me. Do you see me?*

I ached for his love. Couldn't he love me even though my attempts to please him through obedience failed? Nothing I'd been taught from sermons or Bible studies or this missions group ever revealed any other solution than to strive harder. I finally fell into a restless sleep, still clutched by the hopelessness of my inability to please Jesus.

Waking early, I longed to unknot my tangled thoughts by writing in my journal, so I grabbed it and my Bible and hiked to a bench on a grassy hill overlooking the island. The sun's welcome heat soothed me, and I inhaled the richly floral island breeze. A floppy palm tree shifted overhead.

After pouring out my heart through my scribblings, I soon got stuck, tired of my own whining. I gazed over the gorgeous landscape that reached all the way down to the aqua-bordered shoreline and out past a tiny island to the deep blue. *You are so beautiful, God.*

He loves me, I told myself, struggling to banish the image of Jesus shaking his head in disappointment. *No, he doesn't look at me like that.*

I picked up my Bible and flipped to the next passage in the book I'd been reading. John 10. "I am the Good Shepherd …" I stopped reading and pondered those words. *He loves me like a shepherd loves his sheep,* I thought. *I am his sheep.*

I somehow remembered that a shepherd would hold a lamb with a broken leg in his arms. He'd carry the weak sheep until it healed. How I wanted to be that lamb, safe in my loving Shepherd's arms.

Imagining what Jesus might say to me, I wrote, *Ocie Anne Little Lamb, I love you.* But I couldn't write anymore. My hand trembled too much.

What? What did you call me?

I examined the words I'd written. *Ocie Anne Little Lamb.*

Me? I sucked in a heaving breath. *Me?*

I knew these weren't Jesus' actual words. I wasn't an apostle or prophet, but by his providence, in that moment, they were true.

The Bible called us sheep. The sheep of his pasture. The ones whom the shepherd led in the astonishing Psalm 23. Why not Ocie Anne Little Lamb? How I clung to that name! It went against all the works-oriented and performance-based acceptance I'd ever embraced, but I didn't care. The first stirring of freedom I'd experienced for years was kindled by my new name. I wouldn't let it go.

"You look different," my friend commented as I slid next to her at the breakfast table. "Lighter."

"Yes." I tipped my head to the side and tossed her a silly grin. "I'm a lamb. Ocie Anne Little Lamb."

Together we rejoiced in my new name.

Wiping the sticky spot—probably jam—from the kitchen island, I assessed the whole kitchen. A disaster. The surge to be a responsible, capable housekeeper burbled, but how could I clean the layers of soiled dishes and cluttered counters? I was too tired and weak.

But I was able wipe that one spot.

Performing that simple task shooed away the fear that encroached.

Maybe I'd never be "me" again, not the me from before, but did I really want that girl to come back? The tired, lonely, over-whelmed, overly focused toiler? If I lived through a cardiac arrest, came back from the dead, and ended up exactly the same … well, that would be dumb. I had embraced so many of the changes—the new, more intense love toward my family and from Jesus. Resting embraced. My fresh appreciation for life and life's blessings.

I needed to embrace the new weaknesses too. Before my death, I had edged back into finding my identity in what I did, not in Christ. I relied on myself, forgetting that without Jesus I could do nothing. How did I forget that?

I folded my hands on the freshly wiped counter and peered out the window at the spiking cedars across the street, noticed sun specks reflecting on their needles. The path leading to the park where I'd spent so many hours with my kids, swimming, playing,

laughing. I would traipse down that trail again, and maybe ˌˌˌ--
ciate those moments more than I had before. Yes, definitely. *I may never be the same, but the love will be even greater. Won't it, Lord?*

My new weaknesses—lack of energy, requiring so much rest, memory loss—brought me back to being the wounded lamb who needed Jesus to carry her. I rose and wandered outside, gazing at the forest and receiving the cold wind's awakening breath.

I am your lamb still. Carry me, Jesus.

Chapter Nineteen

IMPERFECT OFFERINGS

But he said to me, "My grace is sufficient for you,
for my power is made perfect in weakness." Therefore I will
boast all the more gladly of my weaknesses, so that
the power of Christ may rest upon me.
(2 Corinthians 12:9)

*G*ray light snooped through the blinds as I wearily opened my eyes on the July morning. *No sunshine again?* I yawned. *But the party.*

Before I could focus my groggy thoughts, Abigail bounded into my room. "It's my birthday!"

She snuggled next to me and sprayed me with millions of birthday-related questions. I embraced her as I contemplated getting up and launching into the day.

Finally rising, my energy level sagged as I plodded through the morning, prepping for my big five-year-old's party.

I'm not cut out for birthday parties, I bemoaned as Abigail helped me stir ingredients into the cake batter. A herd of little girls and their moms would expect me to entertain and feed them, and supply oodles of fun. Why did birthday parties feel like a litmus test for mommies?

With a sigh, I plopped the cake in the oven and focused on the other items on my lengthy to-do list.

Forty minutes later, the timer beeped for the cake. Pulling out the chocolate symbol of my child's life, I almost cried. Crooked. Not mildly slanted. One side dipped barely an inch from the bottom of the casserole dish. The other mounded up high and mighty—such a conceited side.

"Ugh," I moaned. Another mom-fail. I imagined the ladies' frowning faces, and worse, I'd let Abigail down. My stomach grinded in anxious tension, but I had to ignore it. Too much to do.

On that same missions trip in which I received my new name, we also traveled to Guam, then boarded a small propeller-driven plane to the most primitive proper island in Micronesia, Yap.

The night before we left, thirty other young people joined me as the missions group's praise band led us in a long, heartfelt time of worship. I lifted my hands, belting out praise, pressing in to God to experience him.

But, as always, my sincere desire to worship was tainted by spiritual pride. *Am I really seeking you, Jesus? Am I just trying to appear spiritual to these people?* A putrid ache lodged in my chest. Would God receive my impure worship?

Even though I relished my new name, Ocie Anne Little Lamb, perfectionism and legalism still chained me, and my awareness of their ugly manifestations became more unmistakable every day. I'd been called out by a leader for judging my teammates for not being passionate enough while doing our skits. How awful I'd felt. She was right. I judged others as I judged myself—harshly, unmercifully.

Staring out the window at aqua-blue waves, I forced myself to press on. *Maybe Yap will be a new start.* As the waves transitioned toward the lush green island below, the plane began its descent. *I will stamp out my pride, Lord. I will serve you.*

Later in the afternoon of the second day in Yap, the leaders told us we would visit the prison. Our group meandered to the building that housed not only the jail but also the post office and the fire station.

Rather than go inside, we filed to the backyard, where the prisoners, all men, waited at tables. A canopy covered the area, but there were no walls or fences. I flitted a look at a friend when I noticed two prisoners slashing bamboo with machetes. "Do you see that?" I whispered.

"They give the prisoners weapons?"

Before we could discuss further, the leaders instructed us to join a prisoner at a table.

I scooted onto the wooden bench next to a young man with straight black hair and a short, stout frame. My friend sat at the table too, but her attention swayed to two guys sitting closer to her. I asked the young man near me his name.

"Mark," he said with an island accent, his high cheek bones remaining still.

After some brief small talk, I simply asked him if he wanted to know about Jesus. He nodded, and then his brown face and almost childlike eyes gazed at me as I told him the simple gospel. You are a sinner. Jesus paid for your sins on the cross. Believe. He asked a few questions, but mostly listened quietly, appearing entranced by the story.

The next day, he came with a few specific questions, and again, as I answered, he peered at me, awe kindling in his eyes. An intense connection to Mark grew in my heart—love, overwhelming compassion, longing for his soul. Yet a calm trust tempered this passion as I peacefully watched what God was doing. In a sense, I observed from the outside, with the angels, waiting to rejoice.

The tropical sun beat down the following day as my team and I tromped in our long skirts and tank tops through the small town toward the jail. My feet had become stained with the red clay that pervaded the islands.

Local kids waved. "Hi, Chicken Ocie!" one said, good naturedly teasing me about last night's skit. I had played the chicken.

I amusedly waved back. Not in the least bothered by that name. Glad to have it.

As we entered the jail and were led to the backyard, a breeze quivered through, gifting the ocean-flower-blended scent of the tropics.

I scanned the covered area until I found Mark, sitting at our usual table, a huge grin on his face. I hadn't seen him smile before, but this smile sent a tingle up my spine.

Sliding into the chair, I tilted my head and waited. He had something to tell me. I thought I knew what it was, but I held my breath, not wanting to presume. Hoping to feel this moment.

"Last night, after lockdown, Ocie . . ." he began. He looked at his hands, but the corners of his lips curved upward. Then he lifted his face, and his gaze connected with mine. "I got out of my bed and knelt down, and I prayed to Jesus. I asked him, 'Will you forgive me, Jesus? I want to live for you. Will you help me, Jesus?'" His white teeth appeared as his face beamed with joy. "And I knew he was with me. Am I a Christian now?" He giggled like a shy child.

I gleefully laughed and held his hands and said, "Yes. Yes, you are a Christian!"

Heaven interrupted, rained down in glorious joy into a tiny island's backyard jail where a prideful, insecure, scared girl sat with a criminal at a table with the island breeze that carried not merely the tropical scents but also the Holy Spirit of God.

I felt like crumbling in praise to God, falling down right there in the red-clay dirt before God's awesome grace, but instead, my brother Mark and I prayed together, giving thanks to our Father.

Even though I gleaned many lessons during my six months on the mission field, I still clung to perfectionism. After I returned from Micronesia, I soon joined the staff of a youth ministry I'd been involved in during my high school years.

As usual, I pursued this assignment with a fervor I hoped would please God. After a couple of months, I established Bible studies at one Christian and one public high school. Each week at the Bible studies, I searched for kids whom I would personally invite to "disciple" with me. Discipleship—a one-on-one or small group where we would go through a workbook together—made up the core of the ministry but not the final goal.

The true measure that I shone as a stellar leader, and thus really loved Jesus, didn't hinge on how many discipleships I had each week, but how many of my students discipled others, moved on toward leadership. This was known as "multiplication." I glued my designs on that goal.

Entering the public high school campus, I dodged a hoarding flock of seagulls that swooped down for stray junk food as kids ate their lunches around the red bricked campus. I strolled toward the Bible study room, amazed to be serving God this way, not wanting to squander the opportunity.

Two of my regular crazy-awesome girls boogied into my path with big hugs. We giggled as we entered the classroom donated by a Christian teacher. To add to their dedication, they'd brought a friend this time. Ally.

"Hi!" I hugged her slim frame as her chin-length ash-brown hair swished. She chuckled awkwardly, but graciously returned a pretty smile. Soon the group of about ten gathered on orange plastic chairs as I shared about being sold out for Jesus. Ally's eyes seemed to ponder what I said. I detected a hunger in her. *Lord, help me to guide Ally closer to you.*

A sweet, friendly, dependable girl, she soon joined the troop of regulars. She was pretty—a dancer—but not stuck up, and kids liked her. I liked her. I soon decided to invite her to disciple with me. The following week I asked her.

A full grin with a touch of relief, like she hoped I'd ask, graced her face. "Sure!"

Later that week we embarked to Burger King for a Coke, fries, and workbook study time.

I appreciated the quick, comfortable connection that formed as we joked and shared. Soon our conversation easily shifted to spiritual things. With Whopper scents drifting around us, we opened our hearts about God, even praying for her twin sister and other friends.

I valued her—loved her—but my appreciation for this precious gift was tarnished by my hunger to succeed. If I managed this well, she might be leadership material.

One week she arrived to the restaurant without having finished her workbook.

"You didn't get it done?" I frowned.

"I'm sorry." Her eyes perked upward, expecting grace from me.

I withheld. Passive disapproval took its place. "Hmm. Well, that's okay. You'll do it next week, right?"

She nodded shyly.

Elbowed between the joyful bonding times, I pressured her. When Ally didn't get her work done, declined to come street witnessing, or failed to attend one of the bigger Bible studies, I judged. I used guilt, passive-aggressive tactics, or blatant pushiness.

Around spring break, the ministry's parent organization held a getaway in Palm Springs. Several of my disciples had signed up, including Ally, and I hoped it would forge a life-transforming event for them. But from the beginning of the trip, something felt unsettled at the getaway. Conflict arose when the kids in my group wore "inappropriate" swimsuits. Embarrassed to have my group seen as "out of line," I gathered my girls around the marble indoor pool.

"You guys need to think about Jesus. Are you reflecting him or yourselves? He wants you to be on fire for him, and what you wear, how you act here, affects how others think about him."

There, that should be strong enough.

"Why does it matter?" Ally, my sweet, adorable friend, rolled her eyes. "This is stupid."

Shocked at her snippy attitude, anger surged. "Do you have something to say, Ally?" I couldn't believe she would betray me just when I needed support.

"I'm so sick of this."

The other girls faded from my view as I zeroed in on Ally. My chest throbbed in painful heartbreaks. "Come with me," I commanded. "Right now."

She huffed to a stand, and I marched her to our room, never relenting in my resolve to rebuke her, through several hallways and elevators. *I've given her so much. She was ungrateful, downright mean to me.*

But as we sank into the peach-decorated couch, tears welled in her eyes. "I can't live up to your standards. I'm sorry." Her hand quivered as she wiped her eyes.

Finally my voice thawed. "What do you mean?"

"Everything is just … I've been trying to do what you want, but I can't do it. It's not … It used to be fun." She buried her head in her hands.

Shame blanketed me. I'd peacocked around like a superdiscipler, like an überleader, like God's special helper. But in that crumbling moment, my success melted away. All my efforts stank with rancid worthlessness—worse, my works felt like sin.

"I'm sorry, Ally." I awkwardly patted her shoulder, so terrified of failure. "I shouldn't have pressured you."

"It's okay," she said and reached for a hug.

As we embraced, my heart cowered in humble amazement at how easily she forgave me, like she accepted me even though she just witnessed my imperfection.

When we returned home, I couldn't accept that she really still liked me. I struggled to even make eye contact, shame so encompassed me. How could I hurt this awesome, beautiful student? I stopped our discipleship meetings. When I saw her at Bible studies, uneasiness chased me from her. I avoided her, afraid she'd hate me, afraid of facing my failure.

To make up for it, I poured myself into the ministry even more. I had to prove myself. It was all I knew to do.

As years passed, I hearkened back to that time as if a shadow of shame still clung to me. I ran from the memory to escape the heartache I'd caused not only Ally, but also others who I'd fed a works-centered message.

But God's grace was greater than my weakness. Like he often does, Jesus took my feeble and crusty clay, mixed with pride and sin and fear, and created shining beauty, beyond what I expected.

About twenty years later, out of the blue, I heard from Ally.

I wanted to thank you for taking the time to ask me to hang out after school. You took me to Burger King and gave me a workbook about knowing God. When I look back at that time in my life, I am so grateful for people like you who helped guide me in my walk.

Sincerely,
Ally

Tears drenched my cheeks when I read this. Oh, the penetrating love of the glorious Maker of life who knows me, calls me his own. The shame I thought chased me wasn't so dark and scary after all. When I finally gazed upon it, I found that I had no reason to fear, not when a transforming God held my offerings in his hands. His sacrifice made my sacrifice acceptable, not because of my worthiness, but because of his. What incredible love is this?

Ally's now a mommy who loves Jesus and teaches dance. Amazing.

That afternoon in July, as I ogled the lopsided birthday cake, Abigail pranced into the kitchen. "It smells so good! Is my cake done?" She peeped at the chocolate treat and squealed. "Perfect!"

Gulping a breath, I threw her the biggest smile I had, my angst melting away. "It is!" Tugging her to my side, I confirmed her assessment. "Perfect!" Later we gleefully decorated the imperfect creation and then excitedly served it to the partygoers at the park. And guess what? No one complained one bit about the crooked cake.

Later, I wrote this on my Facebook page:

Today is Abigail's birthday party. She turned five last week. I was feeling grumbly about how I don't really like preparing for kid birthday parties, but then I thought, I'm just glad to be here for it, and that kinda changed my attitude.

And I snuggled up with my big-girl five-year-old, beginning to glimpse that maybe that's how God works. He takes our imperfect offerings and makes them into parties.

Chapter Twenty

THY WORD

*Your Word is a lamp to my feet
and a light to my path.*
(Psalm 119:105)

For years, I'd inhaled everything I could about Jesus. Not only did I go to church twice on Sundays, but I also read Christian books by famous authors, attended and eventually taught more Bible studies than I could count, finished three summer internships with my youth ministry leader, and even completed a year of college courses designed to train ministers. I craved God and his Word!

But by the time I jaunted away for the Hawaii and Micronesia mission trip, apathy toward the Bible inched in, supplanting my zeal. The same teachings from various sources repeated endlessly. Did the Bible offer nothing fresh? Never anything new? Maybe I'd already learned all there was to know.

During three months of the six-month training, our team suffered for the Lord in Hawaii. This made up the lecture part of the trip, and I hoped to discover some new method or revelation to propel my Christian walk beyond the lukewarm level I worried I'd settled into.

The hum of large box fans' comforting breezes ruffled in the background one morning as I listened to the latest lecturer. He painted a portrait of the most radical-for-Jesus person he knew. This person heard God so clearly that as she strode down the street, God directed her exactly where to go.

According to the speaker, this concept unlocked the secret of truly living a radical life. It was hearing God's voice and obeying. My heart skipped against my ribs. A new concept! I'd pinpointed the answer to pleasing God—listen to his voice.

The next day, after breakfast, I paced out of the hall onto the sidewalk, confident God would tell me where to go, whom to talk to. *I'm here. I want to serve you better, Lord. Please talk to me.*

Breathing in the ocean-fresh air, I strolled around the quaint Hawaiian town, intently listening for instructions, but none came. Panic simmered. What if he wouldn't speak to me? *I must be doing something wrong. I'm sorry for my pride, Lord. Will you talk to me like that radical Christian?*

Still nothing. Disappointment and doubt agitated, threatening to take over, but I cast the feelings aside. I desperately longed to distinguish God's voice, but since yawning silence still pervaded, I decided to follow my instincts. I ambled along, asking, *Is this where you want me to go, Lord?*

Jesus still refused to answer in any distinguishable way. Not even a still small voice broke through, but determined to avoid another failure, I sort of followed my feelings. *Is this what the lecture guy meant by hearing you, Lord? I thought it would be an actual voice.*

I continued my trek until I ended up in front of a gift shop. I lingered there, gaping at the door. *Is this where you want me to go?* Afraid that if God expected me to step inside and I didn't, he'd frown on me, I opened the door.

It jangled, and I surveyed the beautiful products—flowy

handmade clothing, blown glass, and watercolor pictures. A gorgeous woman, tall and slender with short hair, greeted me with an exotic accent.

Oh, Lord, am I supposed to witness to her? "I … um … think God brought me here." As soon as I said it, embarrassed dread smacked me, but I soldiered onward, asking her if she knew Jesus. She kindly hazarded to answer me honestly, saying she believed in all gods.

In order to prove that God had really directed me here, to this woman—that he spoke to me and I obeyed—I absolutely had to convert her. Not tuning in to her answers, I barfed out the witnessing phrases I'd learned. I shot out, "Jesus is the only way to heaven. If you don't believe in him, you will go to hell," and other offensive, unloving assaults.

She soon cooled. "If you please, I do not like to talk about this anymore," she said, not angrily but firmly. "If you're not going to buy something, you may leave."

My stomach clenched. "I … I'm sorry."

I departed the shop and plodded home. *What did I do wrong, Lord? I want to be radical for you. I want to hear your voice.*

The rest of the day, my dread of displeasing him swelled. I knew it wasn't his fault I couldn't hear him. Sin must've blocked the signal. My sin. So I continued straining to hear. Would he ever be pleased with me? Enough to speak to me like he did to others?

A few days later, sitting on my bottom bunk, I opened my Bible.

"Woe to you, scribes and Pharisees, hypocrites! For you are like whitewashed tombs, which outwardly appear beautiful, but within are full of dead people's bones and all uncleanness. So you also outwardly appear righteous to others, but within you are full of hypocrisy and lawlessness" (Matthew 23:27–28).

As I studied the palm tree outside my window, I knew I had my answer. Finally, something rang true. Those words perfectly described me. Everyone thought me to be the ideal Christian—both the folks in the missions group and at home where I'd done youth ministry for the last three years. I appeared righteous.

But I knew, and surely God knew, it was fake. Inside was hidden a writhing ball of pride.

Days passed, weeks, in this paradise, while I existed in the harsh reality of my sinful state. *Dead man's bones.* Over and over those words sunk into me until I accepted them as the reality of who I was. A whitewashed tomb with dead man's bones inside. And Jesus, in his perfect justice, condemned me. I deserved to be condemned.

One day, as the late-morning sunshine beat down, I found my way to the beach. Staring at the waves, I cried out to God, not expecting an answer—and not receiving one. So I kicked off my flip-flops and sprawled out on a bed of grass overlooking the water, the cool grass prickling against my naked legs.

I'm not even a Christian, I thought. *If I ever was, I've surely lost my salvation.*

After a few moments, I moved to the rocky border between the grass and the sand, and stared.

Then, finally, God spoke. But not how I expected.

"Hey, Ocie. Whatcha doing out here?" It was John Gangini, the cute surfer guy who was one of our leaders.

I didn't make small talk. I blurted out, "I'm not a Christian. I've lost my salvation."

He dropped his tanned self down next to me.

I explained my torment, and he asked simple questions. "Do you think you ever were a Christian? Did you ever trust in Christ?"

I searched back over the years to Mrs. Lawson's Sunday school class, and also to a time in junior high when I knew Jesus accepted me, loved me like Aslan. How I adored him and trusted his promise to be near. Tears warmed rivers on my cheeks. "Yes, I think so."

"Then you're a Christian, Ocie. He won't let you go."

I tried to argue, but he gently showed me Scriptures—so many Scriptures—promising that he would never leave me, he'd be my father forever, no one could take me from his hand.

Relief washed over me, and as he spoke the Scriptures, I knew, no matter what, Jesus hadn't condemned me. Maybe I was a white-washed tomb with dead man's bones inside, but even that wouldn't separate me from him. He wouldn't leave me alone. John walked me back to the lunch room, and I ate in peace for the first time in many weeks.

That morning, in the midst of my despair, God spoke to me through his Word brought by one of his servants. He chose the message, not me—a message of love and comfort, not commands on where to turn. Much better than that.

All I had done to make it happen was … nothing.

About six months after my cardiac arrest, glorious sunshine dappled through the trees (rare that summer in Western Washington) as Michael, the kids, and I traipsed down a hiking trail. The birds squeaked out their surprising cacophony, and an earthy woodsy smell mixed with a hint of flowery goodness. To add to the peacefulness, we tramped the trail almost to ourselves. Lovely.

"This is amazing," I said to Michael, plodding next to me.

He shifted his gaze to mine and grinned. "Yeah, it is."

I knew our hearts both beat with the same wonder. *Thank you, Jesus, that I'm here to feel this day. To walk this trail.*

Six-year-old Christian had bounded ahead to scout out the path and check for enemies, like any good Jedi.

As Michael scooted forward, Christian paused his mission and hung back. "I want to be with you, Mama."

I presented my hand, and he pressed his sticky, chubby paw in mine.

Farther up, Ben and Gabby, the big kids, raced up an incline on the side of the trail. Abigail watched wide eyed, from the bottom. Her chin quivered. About halfway up, Ben spotted her.

"You want to come, Abby?" He pounced down. "Take my hand. We'll go together."

As we wandered along this path, the Scripture I'd read that morning quivered to mind. "And walk in love, as Christ loved us and gave himself up for us, a fragrant offering and sacrifice to God" (Ephesians 5:2).

Walk in love. That's what we're doing on this hike. A fresh breeze cooled my face as I relished my kids, enjoying God's creation together. *Thank you, Jesus.*

We reached the "climax" of the trail—a nice view of the surrounding hills and city. Then we commenced our journey back. Soon, the kids, having already viewed the sights, grew bored.

"My feet hurt, Mama." Abigail clung to my legs. "Will you carry me?"

"I can't, sweetie." My calves ached. This was the most exercise I'd gotten since the cardiac arrest. Weariness took hold.

Soon the others tossed their complaints in the murmuring stew.

"I'm tired," Christian griped.

Ben glared at him. "No, you're not. I spent all morning weeding. You didn't even help."

Gabby stumbled next to me. "I'm hungry."

Observing our love hike disintegrating into a tromp through Whiny Wilderness, I thought about encouraging everyone to be nice, but my sciatica nerve panged and a sharp pain targeted my right foot. I was more likely to join in the grumbling than lead us out of it.

At that moment, the verse resurfaced. "And walk in love, as Christ loved us and gave himself up for us."

Earlier, I had focused on the beginning. "Walk in love." So lovely! But its root was grounded in the second part, "as Christ loved us and gave himself up for us."

Yeah, giving yourself up for others? Not apparent as we hiked homeward. So rather than grumbling, I prayed for grace to walk in love, not the easy, ponies-and-popcorn kind of love, but sacrificial love like Christ's. Even when I didn't want to.

Sitting in front of my computer later that evening, I realized how God had guided me through that stressful parenting situation. He spoke to me through a passage of Scripture hidden in my heart. I didn't need any other wisdom, only my Father's words.

Night's darkness created shadows around my desk while I pondered how God's Word had guided me throughout the thorny valleys of my life, sometimes convicting of sin, sometimes comforting, always ushering in his love.

My first step on this journey to love like there was no tomorrow meant accepting his forever love for me—believing it, simply trusting his love. Why did I wrench and wrack to embrace this, even now?

I cozied a blanket around my shoulders as, like a familiar scent carries memories, an old insight circled back. Where else but in the sacred words he so generously spoke to me, his child, could I find the fountain of his love? When afraid of the frowning face of God, his wonderful words of life lavished love on me, revealed his smile.

Remarkably, the Scriptures also blueprint how to love others. That day on the trail and always, he didn't call me to this new kind of love without first filling me and then guiding me step by step—with his Word.

Chapter Twenty-One

NOTHING TO PROVE

Be still before the LORD and
wait patiently for him.
(Psalm 37:7)

fter my Hawaii mission trip, when I served full time on staff with the youth ministry, one of my functions was to help lead a team to Tijuana, Mexico. The other leader, Linda, a more mature and experienced lady, had a connection to a small Baptist church there that needed our help. I'd traveled to this lovely church several times before as a student—helping build the pastor a house, street witnessing in town, feeding the kids breakfast before school.

I'd fallen in love with not only the pastor and his two daughters, Mary and Martha, but also the local kids. How I rejoiced as they raced out of their shacks to greet our team when we arrived. When we sang with the kids, joy filled me as they shouted out the words, *"Alabare a mi Señor"* (I will praise my Lord). In no other place or situation did I feel more in sync with my calling.

Now, I cherished the opportunity to help lead a team to my precious Tijuana.

Our next trip would be at Christmastime. Linda and I envisioned a big celebration for the kids, so we set up a time to meet at Toys "R" Us to purchase trinkets for prizes.

A few days before our meeting, a bad case of bronchitis ransacked my body. I ached all over, hacked in tortuous coughing spells. I was sick, truly sick. But, you see, like a riptide always pulling one direction, my works-righteous compulsion to please God had pulled me back into its crushing control. How could I back out of that trip to Toys "R" Us? Other people on staff warriored through terrible illnesses. I would fight through the pain. God didn't need wimpy Christians. He required commandos.

After valiantly shopping for a couple of hours, without even mentioning how miserable I felt, I advanced toward the exit. But with each step, my head grew heavier. I swayed, leaned, lilted. *Lord, help me. I'm trying to fight for you.*

Finally, I blacked out briefly, enough to collapse onto the floor. I quickly pushed myself to my elbows but couldn't stand, so I scooted to the wall and rested there, feeling like a fool.

Linda, who had been checking out, found me. "What happened?"

"I'm sick."

"You are? Why didn't you tell me?"

"I needed to be here."

She placed a cool hand on my arm. "Are you trying to prove something, Ocie? Because others worked through being sick? You don't have to be like them." She brushed back my hair like a mother would, and the corners of her pretty eyes curved upward. "I used to think I had to keep going when I was sick too, but God doesn't make us all the same. You need to rest."

My starved heart soaked in her compassion and wisdom, but a barrier blocked me from truly receiving her words' truth. I, again, had failed God. Like when I strove so fiercely to perceive his voice in Maui, my crack at pleasing him ended with my own foolishness.

Despite Linda's words, I journeyed to Tijuana and played in the cold winter air with the children until I almost blacked out again. It took six months to kick that bout of bronchitis.

Despite my miserable existence, I continued on this wide path for the duration of my year commitment in ministry. But I was burning out. The insurmountable pressure I heaped on myself both physically and spiritually exhausted me. One day toward the end of that time, I slouched in my room at my parents' house. Light sifted onto papers spread out over my bed. I had volunteered to finish this project, but staring at it, I froze, like a stalled car. *I can't do this.*

I never finished that project, and when the year ended, I quit, wanting nothing to do with any ministry ever again. I got a job at a grocery store.

I hadn't shut the door on God … completely. I kept it cracked open, but I played with the idea of quitting church, saying *so long* to the Christian community forever. Maybe I'd ponder God now and then, perhaps a quick chat once in a while, but no more killing myself in ministry to please him. No more!

If you want me, Jesus, you'll have to come after me.

Around that time, a certain handsome young man with dark-chocolate hair to match his eyes, entered my life. We soon initiated a dating relationship, often hanging out at our mutual friend's house.

One night after everyone else had fallen asleep, Michael confided in me. "I do okay on Sundays, but by Tuesday"—his voice hushed with a familiar tenor, shame—"I wonder if I'm even a Christian."

Something like vinegar boiled in my throat as I nodded. *Yes, me too,* I answered silently, afraid to say it out loud. Finally, I touched his hand. "I guess we need to have more consistent quiet times?"

"I guess."

By God's providence, Michael had trudged down a similarly agonizing path to mine. He too suffered burnout, both from ministry and from a relentless works-oriented existence. After a few months, I moved to a friend's house in Orange County to be near him. At the same time as we basked in the beginning flurries of dating, he was stepping out of ministry, like I had. One Sunday morning, after walking out of church, surrounded by the perfectly quaffed people with their Jesus smiles, we sat at lunch together.

"Why do we go to church?" I asked.

He sighed as we ate our El Pollo Loco. After a minute, he softly said, "I love Jesus."

A mourning hit me. I loved Jesus too, at least I wanted to. I missed the loving Savior I'd once known. He seemed many canyons and mountains away.

During this time, I moved again, in with a friend up in Long Beach, about thirty minutes from where Michael lived. On Sunday evenings after I finished my shift in the grocery store deli, he zipped up the 405 to spend time with me. We didn't know that this drive would kick off a complete paradigm shift for both of us.

One night after arriving at my place, Michael plopped down on the mushy gray couch in the dimly lit living room. "Tonight I listened to the weirdest show. *The White Horse Inn.* You'll never believe what the three hosts were talking about."

I placed a plate of mac and cheese on the TV tray in front of him, then cozied up. "What?"

"Infant baptism."

I grimaced. "Who does that?"

"I know! So crazy, I had to find out what these kooks were talking about."

The following Sunday night, he listened again. And the next Sunday. The more he ingested, the more the show intrigued

Michael. After arriving at my house, he would describe their topics.

"Listen to this," he started one evening as we lounged on a cushioned sofa on the back patio. "They say no matter how we 'feel,' God's grace is an objective truth."

Whenever he talked about this show, he used words like "objective truth" and other smart-sounding phrases. I liked that; it challenged me to think. But the content rattled my foundations.

"'No matter how I feel'?" I sat back, eyed him. "So even if I don't feel like he loves me, he still does?" *Don't mess with me.*

"That's what they're saying." He settled back and drew me next to him. Husky clouds shadowed the moon. "He quoted Romans 4:5." He stalked inside and returned with the Bible already open. "Listen. 'And to the one who does not work, but trusts in him who justifies the ungodly, his faith is counted as righteousness.'" He inhaled. "'The one who does not work.'" He shook his head. "'Justifies the ungodly.'" I spotted confusion, like I felt. Something else too. Awe and ... humility.

I wasn't having it. This couldn't mean *that*. Not what Michael thought. I bull's-eyed on one word. "It's says we have to trust. Trust means obey." My voice rang confident, but my gut ached. *I try to obey, so hard. But I always fail him.*

Michael closed his eyes as if striving to recount Michael Horton's exact words. "Trust is falling into God's arms, knowing he will catch you."

I pushed forward, gripped the chair's cool metal rim. "That's bunk. If we don't have to do *anything*, everyone would do whatever they wanted."

He touched my shoulder. Turned to face me. "I can't believe you said that. It's what they said people would say."

I stilled, unmoving and defensive, my mind swirling with objections.

Over the months, our Sunday-night conversations centered on this show. At first, we merely played with the ideas—which clashed so intensely with our own—in an intellectual chess game. "Is what we've always been taught the same thing Paul rebuked the Galatians for? Works-based Christianity?" "Is faith not a work, but a gift?" "Are we really so wicked we can't please God in ourselves?"

I sleuthed that their main message wasn't infant baptism. They hadn't talked about that since the first night. No, grace was their message. Grace. A grace that said that even though sin buried my guilty soul, I was "declared righteous"—another technical term. It meant Jesus paid the legal penalty for my sin, so my account would be wiped clean.

These hosts insisted on a free grace based completely, totally, only … on Christ.

In the midst of all this, on one cool October evening, Michael drove me to a gazebo overlooking the raggedly beautiful cliffs along the California shoreline. With ocean breezes softly stroking my hair, he asked me to marry him. Overjoyed, I said yes, of course. But, as I prepared for the wedding, these questions stampeded through my mind. I ached to believe in what they said, because if I did, then—oh, the thought of this—God would love me, really, Aslan-love me, no matter how I failed.

The day of our wedding passed, and both Michael and I still wrestled with whether we could embrace the kooks' theology. Did the Bible really teach these things? Finally, Michael read one of the hosts' books, *Putting Amazing Back into Grace*, by Michael Horton.

On a late Tuesday evening, we walked into In-N-Out Burger. "I finished Horton's book," he announced as we approached the red-and-white-checkered counter. "They're right, darlin'. The kooks are right."

He interrupted our conversation by ordering, then grinned as we waited for his Double-Double and the rest of our order.

"What?" I asked.

After I picked up the red tray, he placed his warm hand on the small of my back, guiding me to a booth. As we sat, a hint of sympathy curved his eyes. "It's all grace." He slid in across from me. "Even *after* we're saved. Mike's book convinced me."

I whacked his arm. "You're calling him Mike? Like you're some kind of insider?"

"Yep. I'm going to their weekly classes, starting Wednesday."

"Oh, well, you are so cool."

He released a soft chuckle and the empathetic look reemerged. How could he empathize with me? Did this mean his battle with striving was over? A quick wrench squeezed my shoulders. If he was free, I'd be alone in this treacherous battle. *Ocieanna*, I scolded myself, *you should be happy for him*.

"Everything makes sense now." A smile like the glow from a fireplace lit from his eyes and filled his face. "And I've been loved all along."

I wanted to say *stop it!* But my throat clamped shut. I couldn't think, couldn't process.

He munched a fry. "Have you ever thought, I never got it before—verses like, 'We are dead in our trespasses and sin,' and 'The heart is deceitful above all things,' and the one where Jesus says …" He chomped a big bite of his burger and washed it down with his strawberry shake, a bit of pink lingering on the corner of his mouth.

"Michael! Where Jesus says what?" I snapped.

Oblivious to my grump, Michael swallowed. "'It's not what goes into a man, but what comes out that …' y'know, what is it?"

"'Defiles him'?"

"Yeah."

"What about it?"

He gazed directly at me, serious but gentle—that empathy

again. "If our hearts are deceitful, defiled, and, well, dead, how can we ever be good enough?" A wave of relief seemed to wash over him. "I'm completely unable to please God, darlin'. I can't do it." His voice rose excitedly, as if overcome with joy.

Why would admitting he can't please God make him happy?

"Do you see? I can't do it, but he can. He did!" He brandished his shake as if toasting God. *"Sola gratia!"*

"Ugh." I'd learned this meant "grace alone." I scowled. No way was he right. I couldn't rip my fingers from the chains that bound me to my own merit. How could God not expect something in return for his smiling approval? I knew I'd never be perfect, but didn't I have to try? If I let go of striving, I would never receive the love I longed for. Would I?

Months passed. Michael wisely stopped trying to persuade me, giving me time. I still heard him and his new group of friends associated with the radio show—including the hosts themselves—discuss these things. I couldn't allow myself to believe them.

Then one hot August afternoon, we drove from Orange County an hour away to Michael's parents' house in the desert. Michael and his family drifted outside to tour his mom's latest gardening achievements. For some reason—I don't know why—I stayed in. My mother-in-law's plump, well-worn Bible rested on the oak coffee table. Slouching back into the country-blue couch, I picked it up, rubbed a hand over the soft leather, and then randomly opened to Romans. Chapter nine.

"For he says to Moses, 'I will have mercy on whom I have mercy, and I will have compassion on whom I have compassion.'"

Breathing in the hint of patchouli incense, I pondered that for a long time. By thinking I had to work to please him, was I telling God whom to have mercy on? Conviction speared me. How could I tell God what to do?

Cautiously, like I approached something dangerous, I kept

reading. "So then it depends not on human will or exertion, but on God, who has mercy." Without invitation, a verse I'd heard Michael Horton quote on the radio came to mind: "For by works of the law no human being will be justified."

Bowing my head into my hands, I persevered in my skirmish. Didn't I have to do something? Maybe not to be saved, but for God to love me? *Not by human will or exertion. Not by works of the law. This couldn't be right.* I strained to slam that door. *I already decided this, Lord.*

Then a little farther, "But who are you, O man, to answer back to God?"

Just then, the family's fluffy black-and-white cat bounded onto my lap. I could barely acknowledge its presence. Intensity like knights pressing on castle walls gained ground against my will to fight.

Warily, I ventured to open the gate, just a crack. "Maybe I was wrong," I whispered to the cat. Sunshine beat in through the window behind the couch, warming my neck and back. "Maybe it is grace and not works, but …" The thought *I still need to do something* snagged in my throat like an arrow languishing on its bow. I had no more answers.

In came Michael's words, spoken months before. "I can't obey God's law," he'd said. "I can't do it."

I froze in the filtered sunlight, mentally dumbstruck.

Then it broke. My wall crumbled, and I melted onto the floor, before the throne of God, tears billowing from my eyes. "I can't do it. I can't do it. I can't do it."

I understood why joy spilled from Michael when he first imparted this concept to me. Agreeing with the Word that my heart was deceitful, that I fell short of the glory of God, that deep down I was desperately wicked and unable to please God meant I could stop trying. All those years, I'd emptied myself, moiling to please him, but a holy God could never receive my sin-smeared offerings. All those works I had toiled to perform only added to the weight of my sin. They were filthy rags, dead man's bones, chains keeping me in my prideful, self-centered sin.

After the tears, laughter erupted. Why had I been waging this battle for so long? The knights beating on my heart's gate weren't coming to destroy me, but to declare the news. You don't have to fight anymore. The king already won. You are free.

The cat meandered back, rubbed my legs as I stood. "I'm free," I said out loud. "It's grace alone. It really is!" Random laughs escaped as I strolled outside and joined the others. I sidled up to Michael, nestled my head against his arm. With a giggle, I said, just to him, "The kooks are right."

A heaven-breaking-into-life moment, this shift, which was so much more than a change in theology, set me on a new path. A journey in a different direction, away from the works-righteousness trail I'd slogged down for so many years. I still careened back into old patterns at times, but then I knew where to go for peace.

Back to the grace that opened the door to my Savior's love.

In the months after my cardiac arrest, by God's grace I found a cozy resting place, like John on Jesus' chest during the Last Supper. Grace, everlasting love, surrounded me once again.

But too soon September came, and the first day of our home-school co-op, after a relaxing, glorious summer, arrived. I awoke and immediately a tight anxiety entangled me. I loathed the end of that first summer of my new life. Everything had gleamed new and fresh and amazing. Love held me in soothing, joyful arms warming me like the clean Pacific Northwest sunshine.

During the last week, I'd wrestled with my energy level. Cardiomyopathy (heart failure caused by the cardiac arrest) stole my energy at times. This morning, weariness pulled at me, making each of the actions on my to-do list a strain. *Lord, please*, I begged, *please give me energy.* This would be my recurring plea.

I tromped through the kid madness down the stairs to make sure everyone was munching on their cereal, but no, no one was eating, and two pajama-clad misfits hunched over the blue couch, searching the laundry for clothes.

I snapped at them, then continued rushing through the morning, grumping and pushing my tormented kids to hurry. "Do you have your pencil box?" I asked no one in particular as we hurried to the van. "Is it loaded? What about a glue stick? Do you have a glue stick?" I remembered the great glue stick crackdown from the previous year when faulty moms (including me) had not stocked their boxes appropriately. My stomach clenched. "You must have your glue stick!"

Yes, crazy, frantic, anxious mama had reappeared.

Practically shoving my poor fearful babies out the door, I waited impatiently as they climbed into the van, then I made my way to the other side.

Somewhere on that quick trek through our unkempt, dusty garage—from the passenger side to the driver's door—the frustrated intensity melted into sick conviction. *What am I doing to my kids?* They tried their best to obey my crazy demands. None had flipped me any sassy attitudes.

What am I doing to myself? I placed a hand over my galloping heart. Drew in a breath and realized my shoulders were hiked to my ears (almost) and my jaw ached from clenching. *This can't be good for me.*

In that brief moment, impressions of memories flashed toward me one after another.

The intense stress I felt before the cardiac arrest.

My grinding to be productive, efficient.

The anger I wrestled with.

How miserable I was.

Also, the beauty of the last few months. Sock dances. Resting embraced. Waking up to my husband's beautiful gaze. Longing for my kids.

I scooted into the driver's seat. *I don't want to lose that.* I realized that much of the stress that morning sprang from rushing. I vowed to never rush again, then swiveled to the kids, who were buckling up. "I'm sorry, guys. I was cranky this morning, wasn't I?"

"You were crazy, Mama!" Christian blurted out.

"Christian, don't say that," big sister Gabrielle piped in, gazing at me compassionately. "Mama's just tired and stressed because of co-op."

Abigail reached her chubby hand toward me, and I grabbed it. "You were a tad grumpy, Mama, but that's okay. We still love you."

I kissed her hand, marveling at their unconditional love, so much more Christlike than how I'd treated them that morning.

My anxiety burgeoned from a compulsion to prove to myself and the co-op moms that I could still capably perform everything I'd ever done. I'd opened the gates to old performance-oriented tendencies. Would I be loveable if I was weak?

Somehow, rather than berating myself, as I drove, I found that place again, close enough to hear my Savior's heartbeat. Without fear of rejection, secure in his grace—the grace I'd found years ago in my mother-in-law's living room—I rested.

Chapter Twenty-Two

SIDE OF THE POOL

"Behold, your mother."
(John 19:27)

The typical desert sun warmed the church parking lot as I waited for Mom to drive over the gravel to pick me up from my sixth-grade Sunday school class. When she pulled up next to me, I noticed her red lipstick matched her fingernail polish, as usual, but why was she wearing one of her sharp work suits? I approached the car, and she rolled down her window.

"I guess I should figure out what this church is all about." She answered my unspoken question. "Wait here while I park."

For about three years, she had transported me to the tall stucco church with its burnt-orange roof, dropped me off, and collected me after Sunday school. Neither of us attended the service that followed. Even though I'd gobbled up Bible teachings, asked my best friend Jesus into my heart, and striven to follow him, I'd never participated in an actual worship service.

I don't know what prompted Mom to attend that morning, but as I waited, my thoughts spun in hopeful spirals. Would she come again? Would she learn to love Jesus too? Together we strolled up the outdoor stairs from the classrooms to the chapel.

Her perfume wafted, a comforting scent, as I inched closer to her, waiting for the service to begin. She joined her voice singing hymns about Jesus. She inspected the bulletin, then listened to the sermon. I relished the unexpected and rare time together, especially in this "house" where everything centered on my Jesus.

Each Sunday I wondered if she'd go back, and she did. She never quit. As a child in the 1930s, her parents had herded their nine kids to church, but as an adult she chased after other things, which landed her three marriages and a fair serving of heartbreak. She veered away from God. I didn't know if she ever considered herself a Christian.

Hearing God's Word preached each Sunday ignited her latent faith. Slowly the planted seeds blossomed and bore fruit. Each morning, she rose early to "do her Bible." Sometimes, over breakfast, she'd share with me what God had shown her. I would open up to her as well. At times we even prayed together.

Jesus re-created the distant, uninterested, annoyed Mom I had grown up with, into a generous, joyful mom who loved me—and even liked me.

As I swished past my teen years into my early twenties, the bond between us solidified into a strong friendship. She became my best friend. How we hooted and howled and chortled together! Oh man, she'd become a silly woman. Sometimes she manifested this tendency in embarrassing ways. I always used caution when eating out with her. She had this horrible habit of waiting till others glanced away and then sneakily revealing her mouthful of food to me. She delighted in my feigned frustration.

"Mom! You've got to stop doing that!" I'd say.

"You're right." She'd bow her head as if ashamed. "I won't do it anymore."

A few minutes later, a mouthful of chewed-up food would again appear in my line of sight, followed by more impish tittering.

But that was only one of her mortifying antics. She also loved frolicking around the house naked while my dad shot rubber bands at her—their game, spurred by my mom's silliness. And every so often she'd surprise me by shedding her false teeth and chasing me around the house, bearing her barren gums, and roaring.

As the years winged me away from her, first to college and missions trips, then to my own place, then to married life, I still needed her. I'd call or drop by for any reason. I found a new nail polish, needed advice for a work crisis, or was simply "feeling blue," as she would say. Checking in with her grounded me in unconditional mom love.

Other times I clung to her love in devastating seasons. After I lost my first pregnancy, Michael and I rejoiced in having become pregnant again, but then that little soul passed away too.

The day after the required D&C, which scraped the remains of my baby from me, she poked her concerned face into my tiny, messy bedroom. "Can I come in, Ocie?"

Sobs burst out at the sight of her. "Come in, Mom." I could barely choke out the words.

She stepped in bearing a bouquet of flowers. Cramps squeezed my abdomen and grief tore at my heart.

"Hi, honey." She searched for the perfect place for the vase of daisies, finally settling on the top of the TV. "How are you doing?"

From my spot still in bed, she looked sallow and thin but still joyful. She had recently fought colon cancer—had lost several internal organs—but they said she was cancer-free, so she, in her determined and funny way, decided to put that "behind" her. Still, she didn't appear completely well yet.

Settling beside me on the bed, she fingered the hair from my forehead. "I'm sorry this happened, Ocie." She reached down and hugged me, letting me weep in her arms.

Not long after that we found out her cancer was back, more aggressive than before.

About eight months after my cardiac arrest, Ben and I still hadn't discussed—at least not fully—his memories from the night he watched his mom die. The school year approached, and a generous friend had gifted us money for school clothes, so we decided a shopping trip might present the opportunity to talk.

After meandering through the mall, hoping to decipher what kind of clothes a sixth-grade boy should wear to fit in (but not stand out too much), we roamed to Wendy's for burgers.

"Are we going to talk, Mom?" Ben asked as we pulled into the parking lot.

"Do you want to?"

He nodded and his blue eyes rounded. "Why don't you go through the drive-thru. We can eat in the car and talk."

"Good idea."

So in the Wendy's parking lot, as we scarfed burgers and fries, he very articulately shared his story. We wept together, hugged, and in the end, rejoiced. I asked him to write down his story, so we would always remember. This is what he wrote:

I run up the stairs as fast as I can, thinking you are going to die. I race into the room, hand Dad the phone, and just start crying. I stand at the door, watching Dad doing CPR as the 911 people tell him what to do. I'm really worried. Really stressed out. I stand in front of the bed thinking, *What's wrong with Mom? What happened to her?*

And then Dad says, "Go downstairs! Clean all the hallways and close the kids' doors. Unlock the front door." I know he wants to make sure the paramedics can get in, so I unlock every single door. I even open the garage door.

I see one truck come, then two, then three, until about nine ambulances park on our cul-de-sac. All these people rush in and run up the stairs. I try to look into your room, but I'm too sad. I can't take it.

I go downstairs and sit on the green couch, then move to the chair, just praying, "God, please help my mom to survive. I love her so much. What am I going to do without her? What will we do without Mom? What will the little kids do?"

Then I run back upstairs and try to look again, but it's too much for me, so I go to the couch to get out of the way and cry and cry. Then I start pacing through the kitchen and family room, saying every memory verse I can remember to help me be comforted.

And then on this gurney they carry you down the stairs. When I see you, I think you are dead. I don't know what's wrong with you. They take you out the door, and I think I'm never going to see you again. And then everybody leaves, and it's really quiet.

The sights, smells, and sounds still impacted Ben even months after the tragic night. When for no reason, at twelve years old, he would pat my hand in public, or lovingly stroke my back, or hold a glance a tad long and then say, "I love you so much, Mom," I knew the driving impact of nearly losing me still affected him. Even now, at fifteen, he still sometimes sprinkles me with gratuitous affection. Although he may not consciously realize it, I believe somewhere an appreciation for my life—my simple presence—motivates these offerings.

I've read Ben's story to many MOPS (Mothers of Preschoolers) groups I've spoken to. Even though I give a "you might cry" warning, many cheeks moisten with tears. After a few of the MOPS meetings during which the moms wept, I asked myself why. Why does it matter that I almost died? Why do these ladies cry that Ben almost lost me?

I'm just a mom. I wash dishes. Drive kids around. Seek to discipline with love, but mostly fail. My hair is usually in a soccer-mom ponytail. My jeans often have food imbedded in them. My house never gets clean. I forget things. I'm nothing but a mom. Just a mom.

I puzzled through those questions for a long time. I knew that, objectively, it's sad for a child to lose his mother, but me? Not a great example of a mom, I failed in multiple ways every day.

The answer didn't reveal itself till months later.

<hr>

The cancer we thought we'd beaten in my petite mom's body proved too strong for her. Quickly, too quickly, she deteriorated. I spent as much time as I could with her during those last few months. Once I took her shopping.

"You smell good, Mom," I mentioned as I helped her into the car.

"I'm wearing my expensive perfume, Giorgio." She always said "Giorgio" with a French accent, as if it was the most exquisite luxury a lady could possess. "May as well use it." She half-chuckled, then held my gaze.

Grief tapped against the glass. "I suppose you're right."

As we gingerly straggled through the dimly lit mall, I mentioned that I needed a watch. Inside, I hoped she would buy me one. A memento.

She considered me as if I were a small child asking for a toy, then grinned. "Sure, honey. Why not?" Being her frugal self, she marched me to Target's watch rack.

I chose one that cost thirty dollars, and she balked.

"Thirty dollars for this watch?"

I gazed at her, and then we both laughed at the irony of worrying about thirty dollars when in a blink she'd have no need for money. She bought me the watch, now a keen reminder of our last shopping trip together.

Less than a month later, she lay in the hospital bed that hospice had delivered, unable to walk on her own. I recused myself from work to be with her.

"Hey, Mom," I said.

Her big brown eyes, now sunken into her skeletonlike face, sparkled with joyful recognition. Welcomed by my mom, embraced in her love, I slid into the bed and rested my head against her, taking in her smell, even now faintly of Giorgio, and feeling her touch, listening to her heartbeat.

"I love you, Mom."

She smoothed my hair. "Oh, my Ocie, it's been a joy being your mom. Trust Jesus, okay?"

"I will. Don't worry."

Later that evening, she fell into a coma. The next day, she went to see her Jesus.

Grief attacked in harsh blows at first, then it became a naked tree outside my window. Pointed branches stabbed with raspy whispers of my loss. As months went by, I floundered without her. Driving home from work one night, I decided not having Mom was like swimming in a pool but never being able to touch the side.

That's it, I thought, deflecting relentless sobs. *She was the side of the pool.* I could go out, do my thing, embrace life, succeed, fail—it didn't matter. I always swam back to her to catch my breath. Her ever-accepting love welcomed me, reassured that it was okay to be me. Filling up with her confidence in me supplied courage and strength to plunge back in.

When she died, I lost the side of the pool. No matter what happens in life, I can never refill like I did with her. I've been blessed with many wonderful women who have stepped into my life as "moms," but none of them are the side of the pool. None could be. Only my mom.

❧

One night, about ten months after my cardiac arrest, I lay in bed watching TV. Michael worked late, and I'd given good-night huggies and sweeties to the kids. As I drifted toward rest, the sound of my door opening jolted me to wakefulness.

"I'm opening it a crack, okay?" Ben's gaze narrowed as he waited.

"Sure."

His shoulders relaxed. "Thanks." He disappeared down the hall.

When Michael wasn't home, Ben needed my door open, not so I could protect him, but so he could hear me if the rasping coughs of death sounded again. So he could save me.

Lying back in bed, the weight of my boy's emotional load pressed on me. Again the question rumbled. *Why does it matter if Ben loses me?* Somehow, as the TV light flashed against the wall, the answer came.

I'm the side of the pool for Ben.

I flipped off the TV and pushed up. *Lord? What are you telling me?*

I'd diminished my mom job because I believed I fell short. Because how could doing dishes or caring for a scuffed knee or all my other chores matter? That night I realized I was much more important than I thought. In fact, being a mom wasn't a job at all— it was a calling. No one else could be the side of the pool for my kids but me.

Me?

The concrete knowledge of my worth as a mom cemented in

212

my heart. Knowing this—that I was the side of the pool—poured value on every aspect of my mom identity. A desire to love my kids like there was no tomorrow chased through my soul, and I knew it would transform my very essence.

Joy blanketed me as I lay down again, but before I nodded to sleep, one last truth kindled. *This is about you, Jesus. Isn't it?* Could the side-of-the-pool concept not simply reflect my earthly mom calling, but also my heavenly parent's loving care?

My thoughts wound back to Mom. As much as she loved me, Jesus loved me more. He was the ultimate touch point. Mom only mirrored his care. *I'm not alone, floundering in the pool. I have you, Jesus. I have you.*

Chapter Twenty-Three

HOME

For to me to live is Christ, and to die is gain.
(Philippians 1:21)

The miniscule nine-seater airplane soared its way from the bitty airport at Gustavus, Alaska, between the narrow peaks of the jagged yet stunning mountains, no problem. But as we approached Juneau, a thick crystalline fog engulfed the plane. As I peered out the oval window, everywhere my gaze scanned— above, under, to every side—all I viewed was white. At one point, glimmering runway lights peeked through, so I knew we were close, but we didn't land. Why?

I gripped the armrests, my nerves twined as scenarios, mostly of the plane running out of fuel and plunging into the icy Alaskan waters, berated my thoughts. The other passengers freaked too, I assumed, because no one said a word. Human silence, utter, empty—terrified!—claimed that tiny vessel, interrupted only by the engine's morbid hum. Even the pilot remained hushed. I refrained from asking my burning question, how long until we plummet to our death. He needed to concentrate.

I tried breathing, telling myself everything would b
that I was being silly. But the tiny plane, the fog, the sile

Still fixating out the window, like if I could find a clearing I'd guide the pilot to an emergency landing, the initial adrenaline fear made room for a more heart-ripping emotion. *Please, Lord. I can't die now. Not after you spared me. Not after you pulled me back from death's grip. Please.*

I'd come to Alaska to research my book, *Love Finds You in Glacier Bay, Alaska.* The whole spectacular trip, made with my friend and coauthor, Tricia Goyer, was filled with wonders. We spotted puffins, whales, and even bear—up close. The time with Tricia, her husband, and their adorable toddler sparkled with friendship. The people we met in Gustavus, the setting for the book, surprised us with genuine uniqueness and welcoming hearts. The sheer beauty of the gleaming glaciers, the riveting sky, the shimmering waters. God was near.

But beneath it all something else embraced my heart, like on the morning of the women's retreat—an awe over being there, alive to witness this glorious place. The gift of consciousness embraced me in a heavenly longing.

All my life I'd struggled to believe God really loved me. I felt rejected, not good enough. I strove to please him, only to fall into even more abysmal craters of sin. I agonized in my efforts to be the perfect Christian, the "together" parent, the excellent wife—all to make him love me.

But he always did. In each event I recorded in this book, His love ever lingered close. Better, he himself stayed with me, gently guiding, rebuking, shepherding, comforting, delighting in me. But I chose to run all around his love instead of into his arms where he wanted me to be, even in my failures.

As the gravity-defying piece of metal—which held my mortal destiny, my lifeblood, my existence in its belly—circled through the northern sky, I pondered the last ten months. How Christ opened the gates of his love to me, and somehow, perhaps because of death's scrape, I had received it.

Remembrances opened, breathing on me like Aslan's breath. The time over the summer when I'd relaxed beside Michael, traveling home from a trip to the Washington coast. The kids sat in the back, reading or listening to their music, and as we drove over a sprawling bridge, the beauty of God's creation—the gentle white-capped glimmering river, the sunshine melting into the horizon—that grateful-to-be-here love stirred my heart again.

Another time, this amazement came over me while I worked on my novel at Starbucks, contemplating the rain and pondering a word choice. The writing thoughts drifted away, replaced by wonder. *I'm here. Alive. Thank you.*

This thankfulness-inspiring breath also warmed my soul during the community Easter egg hunt at our flower-arrayed neighborhood park. Beholding my little ones giddily racing to find their eggs, I cradled the moment. *I get to see this.*

Again, on a date with Michael, tucked next to him, watching music videos on YouTube. This new life lust overwhelmed me.

Leaning my forehead against the cold window, I sank into the basketful of memories. Remembering these (and more) moments of beauty humbled me. Each one illustrated God's runneth-over love toward me. His goodness shone over me like rays of gleaming sunshine amidst this frigid flight.

As the airplane wound around yet again, I clung to those moments, holding them like a child presses a favorite book to her chest. *Please, Lord. I'm not ready to leave. I cherish these gifts, the ways you've shown me your love. Will you take them from me?*

Probing out the window, I should've seen it. But my faulty thinking lay veiled as if behind the icy whiteness. I didn't actually realize Jesus' latest lesson till years later—as I was writing this book, actually—but it hung there as engulfing as clouds.

The transcendent memories and all the gifts of the previous ten months sparked an awe-filled contentment. Yet they happened not to make me cling more tightly to this world. Like C. S. Lewis' example of children "fooling about" making mud pies in a slum when they could have a "holiday by the sea," this world's gifts (even though from him!) would never fully satisfy.

When I examine my desire for those present joys, when I truly dig, I don't uncover the fulfillment I long for, but a loneliness for home. Even the joy of knowing his love in these present circumstances—even that—merely hints at the consuming love I'll feel when I see his face and he wipes every tear from my eyes. Now I see in a mirror dimly …

At our homeschool co-op, we are given hymns to learn. A lot of school work in our home takes place on the couch, so sometimes we sit and sing the hymn together. Not too long ago, I snuggled with my three dear ones. The aromas of coffee and scrambled eggs drifted from the kitchen as we sang "My Jesus, I Love Thee." But when we reached the last verse, my voice stalled, struck with the words.

In mansions of glory and endless delight
I'll ever adore thee in heaven so bright
I'll sing with the glittering crown on my brow
If ever I loved thee, my Jesus 'tis now.

Abby tenderly palmed my hand to comfort me. Gabby snuggled closer. Christian grinned sympathetically.

After the hymn finished, Abigail nuzzled in, her silky brown hair smushed against my arm. "Why did that one make you cry, Mama?"

I traced a line down her still-pajama'd arm as I pondered that. "I think heaven makes me cry."

"Because you almost went there?" Gabrielle spoke in her peacefully content voice.

"Maybe."

Christian crossed his legs as he huddled on the floor. "A lot of hymns talk about heaven, I've noticed."

"Yeah. Why do you think that is, sweetie?"

"People back then, when the hymns were written …" Gabrielle tilted her head to look at me. "Do you think they sang about heaven because they were afraid?"

"I bet it made them not as afraid, right?" I said. "It's kind of weird, but knowing Jesus is preparing a place for us makes living here better."

As I continue to remember that white-packed flight and my ponderings around it, this concept of the last verses of hymns grows. The key to love like no tomorrow is the "no tomorrow" part.

Each moment in this life is a treasure. How I've learned this! In so many ways, which I've tried to share in these pages. But paradoxically, this life's sweetest songs ring in even more melodic joy when I remember that they echo my future home.

I can't think about heaven without drawing close to the one who paid the highest price for me to join him there. Sin's dark death separated me from him, but love—a fierce, cross-deadly love—breathed life into me.

How blessed I am that he drew me from that hospital-bed tomb as a reminder of my spiritual rebirth. That resurrection ignited a life-transforming journey of love, worth the cardiac arrest, so worth it.

But another truth occurs to me, one that's been just under the surface all along. One that always whispers to me, giving me hope.

Because he lives, I live.

Oh, they killed him and sealed that tomb, but death couldn't keep him in the ground. He rose!

And isn't it amazing! Because he lives, this life overflows with love like there's no tomorrow. The strength to love, and receive love, and rest in his love, and heaven's gates open up to me. He's not in that tomb. He's not far away. He's not a cruel and demanding father, quick to punish, easy to frown.

Because he rose, I can go to heaven. Because I have that heavenly hope, this life gleams with heavenly joy. Incredible, isn't it?

Oh, how he loves me.

And, friend, he loves you too. Like there's no tomorrow. Will you receive his love?

> *For I am sure that neither death nor life, nor angels nor rulers, nor things present nor things to come, nor powers, nor height nor depth, nor anything else in all creation, will be able to separate us from the love of God in Christ Jesus our Lord.* (Romans 8:38–39)

EPILOGUE

*A*t speaking engagements, I'm often asked a few recurring questions. I thought it might be helpful to answer those questions here. (Note: I'm not an expert on these conditions, just passing along what doctors have told me.)

Are you okay now? Yes! I am tired at times, and I can't exercise as easily as I did before, but the good news is medication manages my condition very well. Other than the low energy, I'm a healthy girl.

What is the defibrillator you describe? You've seen on TV when they shock a person's heart back to life? I have one of those implanted in my chest. If I were to have another cardiac arrest (which, as of 2015, I haven't—praise God!), it will shock me. It's 99 percent effective. A statistic I can get behind!

What is the difference between a cardiac arrest and a heart attack? A cardiac arrest (technically, sudden cardiac arrest) is when the heart ceases functioning, causing the heart as a whole to stop. A heart attack is when blood flow to the heart is blocked.

What caused your cardiac arrest? The doctors told me they don't know what caused my arrest. There is no history of heart disease in my family.

What did it feel like? I don't remember anything from the whole day before the arrest happened. I didn't feel anything until I woke up. In other words, there were no warning signs.

ACKNOWLEDGMENTS

The ones who saved my life. How can I ever thank you?

- Michael, who pumped my chest, keeping blood rushing to my dying brain.
- Ben, who raced down the stairs, grabbed the phone so Papa could call 911, and then paced the house, praying for me.
- The 911 operator, who talked Michael through CPR.
- The paramedics, who rushed to my home in minutes and used their skills and equipment to resuscitate me.
- Jesus, the Lord of life, who by his kind providence allowed me to experience death and resurrection. I give my life forever in thanks to you.

Those who helped with this book.

First, thank you, Michael, for all the editing, rereading, clarifying facts, and kid-watching you did. You saved my life, and without you I couldn't have written about it. Ben, Gabrielle, Christian, Abigail—my wee ones. I know it wasn't easy when Mama disappeared to work for many days, evenings, and Saturdays. Thank you for supporting me with your sweet smiles and hugs when I came home. You kept me going.

Thanks to Carlton Garborg, my old friend, who said yes and squeezed this book into the lineup and supported me along the way—especially thanks for the awesome jokes. Thanks to David Sluka and the team at BroadStreet. To Steve Laube, my agent, for the long conversation and also for welcoming me onto the team. Thanks especially to Mick Silva, who edited his heart out on this project. You challenged me to be a better writer and a better Christian, even guiding me down a path of healing. You went above and beyond, and I am very grateful. Thanks to Janet Grant for your help in the early stages of this book and to Tricia Goyer, who first suggested I write it. A huge—huge!—thanks to my McCritters, Dawn Kinzer and Annette Irby. You read some of these chapters multiple times and always came up with spot-on suggestions to make it better. Your encouragement and friendship mean more than I can say. And thanks, Annette, for coming up with the subtitle.

To my early readers, Alice Hamstra, Anna DeBord, Carol Perlot, Heidi Dalrymple, Jeanie Killion, Stephanie Prince, Stephanie Johnson, and Mary Starman, for your helpful suggestions, enthusiasm, and especially for honestly sharing how my journey touched your lives. To my Northwest Christian Writers Association family. You all rock!

To Lonnie Fravel and Darryle Smith of Exodus Productions, who shot the cover photo of this book and filmed an awesome commercial of my story for Medi-Share—who I also thank for providing an alternative to insurance that relieved us of a huge financial burden.

To Pastor Dan McManigal and the members of Hope Presbyterian, who have prayed me through this journey. You let me be me, and I'm so grateful for that.

To all the people in the pages of this book who contributed to my life in an abundance of ways. You showed Christ's love to me.

To my faithful Savior, Jesus Christ, who guided me through every step of this writing journey, faithfully opening my heart to the truths to share and surrounding me with your love. Without you I'm nothing.

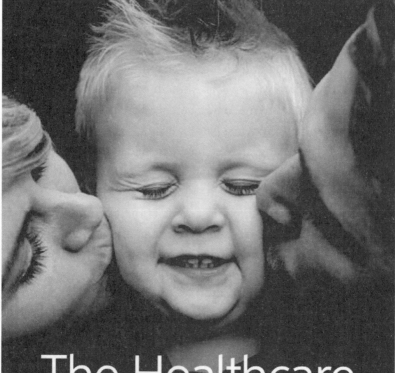

The Healthcare Choice Christians Can Believe In.